The Cruise of
The Alerte

The Cruise
of
The Alerte

E. F. KNIGHT

Introduction by Arthur Ransome

GRANADA
London Toronto Sydney New York

Granada Publishing Limited
8 Grafton Street, London W1X 3LA

First published 1890
This edition published by Granada Publishing 1984
Reprinted 1985

British Library Cataloguing in Publication Data

Knight, E. F.
   The cruise of the Alerte.
   1. Alerte (*Ship*)   2. Voyages and travel
   3. South Atlantic Ocean
   I. Title
   910'.09163'5   G540

ISBN 0-246-12312-5

Printed in Great Britain by
Billing & Sons Ltd., Worcester

CONTENTS

LIST OF MAPS

INTRODUCTION

EDWARD FREDERICK KNIGHT came of a west-country family, but was born in Cumberland on April 23, 1852, the son of an old soldier who had fought through the Carlist war on the staff of the Spanish Legion, had led a romantic expedition into the Caucasus to help the Circassians against the invading Russians and, in retirement, devoted himself to astronomy and mathematics.

Knight's own earliest memories were of Touraine, whither his father had moved when he was about two years old. He was thenceforward bilingual, and throughout his life could be mistaken for a Frenchman by Frenchmen. The family lived at Tours until the bursting of the embankments of the Loire and Cher in 1857 sent the waters raging through the streets, when they were rescued by boat from the second storey of their house. Leaving Tours, they passed through Paris, where they saw the triumphal march of French troops just home from the Crimea, returned to England and settled for some years in Bath, where his father found friends in other retired warriors, among them an old admiral who had fought at Trafalgar and still wore knee-breeches, silk stockings and buckled shoes.

After an unfortunate experience of a Dotheboys Hall at Weston-super-Mare, he was sent to a day school in Bath, where he did so much fighting, fell from so many trees, and damaged himself so often, that he earned the nickname of "Bloody," which he had to explain to his father, who wanted to know how it was that he had overheard some of his son's schoolfellows talk of himself as "Old Bloody." By the time Knight left Bath for Westminster (where, by climbing up the gateway in Little Dean's Yard, he was able to do much midnight exploration of the roof of the Abbey) his father had moved back to France and settled at Honfleur. A mistaken diagnosis of consumption (Knight decided afterwards that he must have broken a small blood-vessel in trying to swim too far

under water) cut short his time at Westminster, and he enjoyed a long interval of private tutoring before he went up to
Cambridge. All his spare time was spent in walking. He
used to save his pocket money, and reckoned that he could
cover the expenses of two hundred and fifty miles of walking
for every pound he saved. "One could live in absolute luxury
on the roads of France in those days on two or three francs
a day when a bottle of good wine cost twopence and a Petit
Bordeaux cigar could be bought for one sou." Travelling light,
sleeping most nights in the open, he walked through Normandy
and Brittany, along the banks of Loire, Rhone and Garonne,
through Burgundy, Savoy, Dauphiné, Auvergne and Provence,
through Piedmont and Lombardy, crossing and recrossing the
Alps through little known passes and more than once losing
himself in the snows. He was eighteen at the time of the
Franco-Prussian War. He walked twenty miles from Honfleur
to Lisieux to volunteer, was rejected as a foreigner and walked
the twenty miles back again without telling his father where he
had been. He was in Honfleur when the Germans marched
in, whereupon he characteristically set off on a walking tour
through the occupied country, noting with some surprise that
he was never asked for his passport by either French or
Germans. Walking into Lyons, when that city was still held
by the Communards, he stayed a week in workmen's lodgings,
saw a good deal of them and noted that "despite their views
which were detestable to a born Tory like myself, they were I
found a very decent lot of fellows." His last walking tour
before going to Cambridge cost him fifteen pounds. On that
small sum he took train to Lyons, walked to Marseilles, took
a deck passage to Algiers, walked to the edge of the desert,
made friends with a mixed lot of French soldiers, without
officers, marched with them two hundred and fifty miles south
to the last French post on the caravan route to Timbuctoo,
went off alone through the Khabyle country, had his first of
several experiences of being arrested as a spy, and made his
way back to Honfleur, where, blackened by the sun, half-
starved and in rags, he thought it better to reach his father's
house at night, sleep in the garden and come in with the milk

in the morning so as to spruce himself before meeting his family at breakfast. Few freshmen in those days can have gone up to Cambridge with so much mixed experience behind them.

At Cambridge he "worked in turn on the mathematical, law and moral science triposes," but presently decided to be content with an ordinary degree, "having wisely come to the conclusion that vacations were better spent in wandering under the skies than in reading for exams." At the same time his passion for walking was superseded by a passion for boats. "Rob Roy" MacGregor visited Cambridge to found a branch of the Canoe Club and preach "Rob Roy" canoes. We have forgotten now how large a part MacGregor and his books (*A Thousand Miles in the Rob Roy canoe*, etc.) played in the sudden growth of interest in small-boat cruises as distinguished from mere racing. The Rob Roy, that frail contraption that allows a man to propel himself as a water spider or sail himself as a nautilus, set many young Englishmen exploring the rivers of the Continent. Knight, returning to France for his vacations, took a Rob Roy with him. C. S. Jerram, who married his sister, bought another and together, like the famous *Arethusa* and *Cigarette* of *An Inland Voyage*, they travelled on the rivers of France, though much more extensively, exploring the Seine, the Rhone, the Saone, the Allier and the Loire.

Canoes were only a beginning. Knight bought a small open sailing-boat, and taught himself seamanship in the unkind water of the Seine estuary, where he learnt painfully that it was not safe to set sail from Honfleur at low water and be overtaken by the tremendous Bore of the Spring tides. After his father's death, he came, when he was twenty-one, into a small private income, and he was still at Cambridge when he bought his first yacht, the *Ripple*, a 5-ton yawl. Sailing for the most part alone, he explored the Channel and the West Coast of France, learned navigation as well as seamanship and was ready for longer voyages.

After leaving Cambridge, he read law, and was called to the Bar, but presently decided that he would prefer a more adventurous career. Russia and Turkey were at war, but no newspaper was willing to send him out as correspondent. An accidental meeting with a friend brought him an invitation to accompany an artist to Albania, and he came back with the material for his first book, *Albania and Montenegro*. He was presently fooled into taking part in a scheme for a new magazine, his withdrawal from which led to a challenge to a duel from the promoter. Knight accepted the challenge, said that as challenged he had the choice of weapons and chose pistols. His opponent refused to fight with pistols, whereupon Knight suggested scythes, as weapons likely to be equally unfamiliar to both parties. There was no duel.

He was twenty-eight when, after a fish dinner at Greenwich, he and a friend watching the busy traffic on the river suddenly made up their minds that they were tired of town and would buy a small vessel and put to sea. They bought the *Falcon*, a 28-ton yawl, collected two volunteers (briefless barristers like Knight himself) and a cabin boy, sailed from Southampton for South America in August 1880, and were away for nearly two years. The result was *The Cruise of the Falcon*, an account of their ocean voyaging, their five months' cruise up the rivers Parana and Paraguay and their long ride over the Pampas. The book found readers at once, and Knight thenceforward had no difficulties in selling anything he wrote. This was fortunate, as on coming back to England after leaving the *Falcon* in the West Indies, he learned that a rascal of a solicitor had made away with most of his patrimony, so that he now had to write not merely for pocket money, but for a living.

Meanwhile, he was always ready to throw himself into any adventure that offered itself. A plan to fit out a brig, load her with trade goods, take her to New Guinea, make a settlement there, get concessions of land "by purchase or otherwise" from the savage natives, peg out claims over mineral deposits and float a company, had gone a long way (the brig was already loading in the Thames) when Lord Derby denounced the "gentlemen adventurers" as buccaneers and the Government "put a stop to our expedition." Deprived of the chance of becoming a New Guinea conquistador, he wrote the first of his several novels. Though nobody could tell a neater anecdote, he was a dull novelist. There is, however, in one of

his impossible love stories a lively passage describing the death
of his hero, a briefless barrister and philosopher (very like
himself) who in despair burns the great book he has written,
sails out through the Needles in a five tonner (very like the
first *Ripple*), and crosses the Channel in a gale to find a satisfactory death among the breakers off the mouth of the Seine.
There, of course, he was more at home than in passages of
sentimental misunderstanding.

In 1885, he visited the West Indies again, this time in a
friend's steam yacht. He borrowed the old *Falcon* at St.
Vincent to take his friends for a sail, only to find that she had
two feet of weeds on her bottom, so that the yacht's launch
had to come to the rescue and tow her into port. Back in
England in 1886, he bought the converted lifeboat that is the
heroine of *The Falcon on the Baltic*, and the following year made
the voyage described in that book. In 1888 he cruised in her
again, had her fitted with lee-boards in Holland and finally
brought her home to the Thames.

When visiting the rocky, uninhabited island of Trinidad in
the first *Falcon* he had known nothing of the treasure supposed
to have been buried there by pirates in 1821, and said to
include the gold candlesticks from the Cathedral of Lima,
removed during the War of Independence. In 1888 Knight
heard of several expeditions, one of them from South Shields,
that had tried and failed to find it, and himself took train to
South Shields, where he heard the whole romantic story (a
Stevensonian tale of the captain of an opium-trader and a
Russian Finn known as "the pirate", with a scar across his
cheek, who had himself taken part in burying the treasure
and when dying at Bombay had given to the captain, in great
secrecy, a bit of ancient tarpaulin with a map of the island).
Knight decided to visit Trinidad again, and did so in the *Alerte*
(56 tons T.M.) with a crew of four paid hands and nine
"gentlemen adventurers," who risked £100 a head. The result
was no treasure, several quarrels, and the very good book here
reprinted.

He came back from Trinidad in February 1890. In the
winter of that year, when he was thirty-eight, Charles Sped-

ding, his cousin, an engineer then building the Gilgit road out of Kashmir, was in London, and invited Knight to come back with him to India, telling him that, besides the interest of road-building, there was the likelihood of a frontier war. Knight saw his chance, went to Printing House Square, talked over his proposed journey with Moberly Bell, and went off with a commission as *The Times* correspondent in his pocket. He had made one reputation as the author of *The Cruise of the Falcon.* He now laid the foundation of another, as war correspondent, doing the work for which so much of his youth seems now to have been a conscious preparation. As always, he took every chance that offered, was not content to see Kashmir, but accompanied Captain Bower to the frontiers of Tibet, crossed and recrossed the Himalayas, took an active part in the Hunza-Nagar War, being twice mentioned in despatches, and came back to England a year later with the material for his book *Where Three Empires Meet.* From that time on he never missed a war if he could help it. On his return from the Himalayas he became one of Henley's young men on the staff of the *National Observer,* but was soon away to Matabeleland for *The Times.* He brought back material for a book about South Africa, where he had seen much of Cecil and Frank Rhodes and Dr. Jameson, but the book was never finished, for he was off again to Madagascar to see the French war from the Malagasy side, as the French would allow no correspondents. He saw the Sudan campaign of 1896, when, finding that camels were being stolen nightly he had all his dyed with purple rings round eyes, neck, legs and tail and a large *Times* clock on each flank. He came home from the Turko-Greek war of 1897 in time to take part in an experimental balloon trip, was in the Sudan again in the same year and missed being present at the fall of Omdurman in Kitchener's third campaign only because, in the Spanish-American war, *The Times* sent him to Cuba. To reach Cuba, then blockaded, he persuaded a friendly ship's captain to put him afloat in a dinghy some miles off the Cuban coast. The dinghy soon capsized, but, as Knight said, she was an excellent sea-boat when full of water. He was able to rest in her, between capsizes, all night, and in the morning, with a favouring wind, he was able to bring her bows up by sitting under water in her stern, to paddle with the only oar he had and to get ashore, losing everything he had with him, and being at once arrested and imprisoned as a probable spy. In the South African war he represented the *Morning Post*, and lost his right arm at the battle of Belmont. He did some general journalism for the *Morning Post*, going round the world with King George V and Queen Mary when they were Duke and Duchess of York, and revisiting South Africa. His passion for boats never left him. He wrote two practical handbooks on the subject, and in *Small Boat Sailing* (Murray) he tells of a cruise in Florida in a flat-bottomed punt, a voyage down the Nile in a *gayassa* and a voyage in an Arab *dhow* from Suakin to Massowah. That book also tells how even the loss of his right arm did not put an end to his sailing. It describes, for the benefit of other one-armed men, the ingenious devices whereby he made his second *Ripple*, a Bembridge lug-boat, into a vessel that he could sail, in the most exact sense of the word, single-handed. Nor did the loss of his arm prevent him from seeing what he could of the Russo-Japanese war, when he was with General Kuroki in Manchuria and complained of lack of liberty. In writing his *Reminiscences*, he grew suddenly impatient, cutting them off short after the Cuban adventure, dismissing the South African war in a single sentence and cramming the last twenty-five years of his life into less than a page. He died on July 3, 1925.

ARTHUR RANSOME

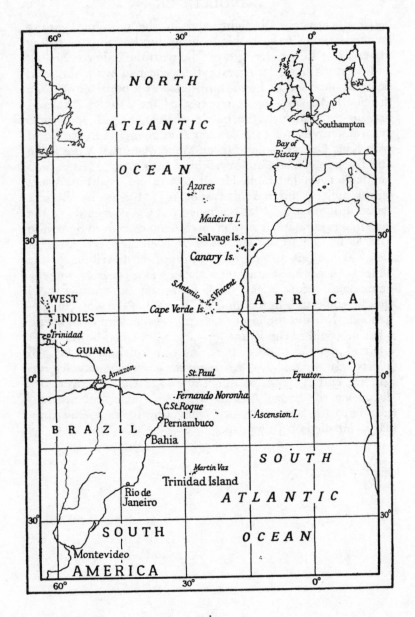

CHAPTER I

THE HISTORY OF THE TREASURE

IN the course of a long cruise in the South Atlantic and up the South American rivers, in the years 1880 and 1881, with my little yacht the "Falcon," I found myself, more by accident than intention, in the neighbourhood of the small desert island of Trinidad. We were bound from Montevideo to Bahia, and, after running before a heavy pampero off the River Plate, we fell in with strong head winds, and had to thrash our way to windward for upwards of a thousand miles of choppy seas and boisterous weather, while the rain poured down upon us almost without cessation, as it not unfrequently does during the season of the northerly Brazilian monsoon.

We steered a course away from the land to the eastward, hoping to meet with more favourable winds when we had obtained an offing of some four or five hundred miles. Vessels bound north from the Plate during the season of the northerly monsoon invariably pursue this plan, sailing as much as seven hundred miles close hauled on the port tack before they go about and make their northering. Thus it was that our course brought us in the vicinity of Trinidad, which lies in latitude 20° 30' south and longitude 20° 22' west, distant about seven hundred miles from the coast of Brazil, and my curiosity being aroused by the description of the islet in the "South Atlantic Directory" I decided to land and explore it.

We came to an anchor off this desolate spot on December 8, 1881, and we remained there for nine days. Our adventures of various sorts, the perils of landing, the attacks made on us by the multitudes of hideous land-crabs and ferocious sea-birds, our difficult climb over the volcanic mountains, and finally our anything but regretful departure from one of the most uncanny and dispiriting spots on earth, are fully set out in my book, "The Cruise of the 'Falcon.'" On turning to that book I find that I state there that I had had more than enough of Trinidad, and would on no account set foot on its barren shores again—a rash resolution which I was destined to break nearly ten years after my first visit to the island.

The descriptions of Trinidad in the "South Atlantic Directory" are all of an old date, and were supplied at different times by captains of vessels in want of water or with crews stricken with scurvy, who effected a landing in order to procure water or the purslain and other greens which abound on some portions of the shore. Halley in 1700, Amaro Delano in 1803, and Commodore Owen in 1822 visited the island, and it is from their accounts that most of the information concerning it has been gathered. All describe the landing as extremely difficult, and often quite impracticable, on account of the almost perpetual surf which breaks on the iron-bound coast. Consequently mariners avoided the coral reefs and sea-worn crags, and, though the masters of homeward-bound vessels from around Cape Horn often sighted the island from a safe distance in order to correct the rate of their chronometers, it was rare indeed that the foot of a human being trod its shores.

But now the land-crabs and sea-birds of Trinidad must be becoming almost familiarised with the sight of man, for the report of a vast treasure that is supposed to have been buried here some seventy years ago, has induced no less than five different bands of adventurers in the course of the last twelve years to fit out vessels for the purpose of seeking their fortunes among the volcanic ash.

This is an account of the most recent of these ventures, and I think it will be the last of them; for whereas all the previous explorers—in consequence of mutiny, the difficulty of landing, and other causes—failed to make any real attempt at digging into the landslip which now covers the spot where the treasure is supposed to lie, and, losing heart in the presence of the preliminary perils and discomforts, abandoned the island after a few days' stay, we succeeded in landing by degrees our tents, tools, and stores, and established quite a comfortable little settlement, while the digging was steadily carried on for three months, and many thousands of tons of earth and rock were removed.

We worked on until we were satisfied that further search
was useless. We failed to find the treasure, but we did what
our predecessors did not—we had a very good try for it; and
we have, I think, at any rate proved that it is not worth the
while of any other adventurers to go in search of this too
carefully concealed hoard.

When I visited Trinidad in 1881 I was not aware that a
treasure was supposed to be buried there, else I should most
probably have prosecuted some preliminary search with the
small crew—we were five all told—and the inadequate tools
I had on board, so as to ascertain whether it would be worth
while to organise a properly equipped expedition on my return home. It was not until the year 1885 that my attention
was directed to paragraphs in the newspapers which spoke of
the departure from the Tyne of the barque "Aurea" with a
considerable company, including navvies, and well provided
with the tools that were considered necessary for the recovery
of the treasure.

These adventurers started full of hope, but were doomed to
disappointment, as is shown in the following extract which I
cut from a daily paper some months later :—

"Further information has been received regarding the unfortunate expedition of the 'Aurea,' the vessel chartered by a
number of Tynesiders for a voyage to the small island of
Trinidad, off the coast of Brazil, where it was reported a large
amount of treasure was concealed. The last letter is from one
of the seamen, a young man named Russell, to his parents in
North Shields. Russell states that it is with *the greatest pleasure*
that he has an opportunity of writing, and continues to say that the
'Aurea' left the island on April 29, and, he was sure, the crew were
not sorry at leaving. He states that eight seamen were ashore fourteen
days, and at the end of that time they were so exhausted with the want
of water and provisions and with the scorching heat, that they had all
to be carried on board. As a consequence eight of them were laid down
with fever, and out of the eight two seamen died. The expedition was
thus unfortunate in more than one respect. The 'Aurea,' according to
the writer of the letter, was at Trinidad in the West Indies, and was
expected to leave for England. Russell says nothing about treasure;

3

the burden of his letter is that the crew left the island with the greatest satisfaction."

This ill-fated expedition of the "Aurea" was, so far as my information goes, the last before that of the "Alerte."

In the autumn of 1888, I happened to meet some South Shields people who knew the history of the treasure and of the previous expeditions. They told me that there had been some talk lately of fitting out another vessel to renew the quest, and that many undeniably shrewd Tynesiders had a complete faith in the existence of the treasure, and were willing, despite former failures, to risk their money and lives in order to discover it. My informant gave me an outline of the evidence on which this faith was based, and I heard enough to so interest me that I forthwith took train to South Shields and put myself into communication with the heads of the "Aurea" expedition, with the view, in case I should consider the prospects of securing the treasure to be not too remote, of fitting out a small yacht and sailing away once more to Trinidad.

The following is the substance of the story as I heard it from Mr. A——, who was the prime mover of the last venture, and who himself sailed in the "Aurea," and passed fourteen days on the island.

"There is now living not far from Newcastle, a retired sea captain, Captain P——, who was in command of an East Indiaman engaged in the opium trade in the years 1848 to 1850. At that time the China seas were infested by pirates, so that his vessel carried a few guns, and a larger crew than is usual in these days. He had four quartermasters, one of whom was a foreigner. Captain P—— is not sure of his nationality, but thinks he was a Russian Finn. On board the vessel the man went under the name of the Pirate, on account of a deep scar across his cheek, which gave him a somewhat sinister appearance. He was a reserved man, better educated than the ordinary sailor, and possessing a good knowledge of navigation.

"Captain P—— took a liking to him, and showed him kindness on various occasions. This man was attacked by dysentery on the voyage from China to Bombay, and by the time the

4

vessel reached Bombay he was so ill, in spite of the captain's nursing, that he had to be taken to the hospital. He gradually sank, and when he found that he was dying, he told Captain P——, who frequently visited him at the hospital, that he felt very grateful for the kind treatment he had received at his captain's hands, and that he would prove his gratitude by revealing a secret to him that might make him one of the richest men in England. Captain P—— says that he appeared very uneasy about this secret, and insisted on the door of the ward being closed so that there might be no listeners. He then asked Captain P—— to go to his chest and take out from it a parcel. The parcel contained a piece of old tarpaulin with a plan of the island of Trinidad on it.

"The man gave him this plan, and told him that at the place indicated on it—that is, under the mountain known as the Sugarloaf—there was an immense treasure buried, consisting principally of gold and silver plate and ornaments, the plunder of Peruvian churches which certain pirates had concealed there in the year 1821. Much of this plate, he said, came from the cathedral of Lima, having been carried away from there during the war of independence, when the Spaniards were escaping the country, and that among other riches there were several massive golden candlesticks.

"He further stated that he was the only survivor of the pirates, as all the others had been captured by the Spaniards and executed in Cuba some years before, and consequently it was probable that no one but himself knew of this secret. He then gave Captain P—— instructions as to the exact position of the treasure in the bay under the Sugarloaf, and enjoined him to go there and search for it, as it was almost certain that it had not been removed. The quartermaster died shortly afterwards."

Now this story, so far, bears a strong family resemblance to many other stories of pirate treasure, mythical or otherwise, and, though there can be no doubt that great stores of valuable plunder are still lying hidden away in this fashion on many a West Indian cay and desert ocean island, the dying quartermaster's deposition was hardly enough by itself to warrant the expense of fitting out an expedition for Trinidad. But on making researches it was found that his story was corroborated in many remarkable ways.

In the first place the archives of Cuba were inspected, and a record was discovered which showed that a gang of pirates who had plundered Spanish vessels sailing from Lima had been hanged at Havannah at the time mentioned.

The probability of the story is further strengthened by the actual history of Peru during the war of independence. It appears that the Spanish population of Lima entertained a wholesome dread of the liberators of their country, and deposited large sums of money and a vast amount of plate in the forts for security. Lima was then a city extremely rich in gold and silver plate, and the value of the property lying in the fortress alone was estimated by Lord Dundonald as at least six millions sterling.

Lord Dundonald, who was at the time in command of the Chilian fleet which had been sent to the assistance of the liberators of Peru, endeavoured to obtain possession of this fortress by negotiations, and offered the Spanish governor to permit his free departure with two-thirds of this treasure on condition of the remainder, together with the fortress, being given up to the Chilian squadron. The admiral hoped by means of this one-third to abate the mutinous spirit of his men, who had received no pay for a long period, and who were, moreover, in a state of actual destitution. But, to Lord Dundonald's disgust, the Peruvian Protector, San Martin, for purposes of his own, allowed the garrison to evacuate the fortress, carrying away with them the whole of these riches. Later on, however, Lord Dundonald took the responsibility on himself of seizing the Protector's yacht at Ancon, and discovered that it was entirely ballasted with silver coin and uncoined gold. With this he paid his sailors some of their arrears of pay and prize-money.

During the first few years of their liberty the unhappy Limenos must have occasionally regretted the old Spanish misrule, bad as it was; for their liberators plundered them in the most shameless fashion, and most of the wealthy citizens of

Lima were reduced to a state of abject poverty. The tyrannical Protector inflicted great hardships on the Spanish inhabitants, and among other of his decrees one was passed confiscating to the public treasury one-half of all their property. When some of these unhappy people, driven to desperation, took to sea and endeavoured to escape with the remaining half of their possessions, the Republican officers boarded their vessels and, wholly regardless of the decree, appropriated this half also.

The wealth of Lima, the richest city of Spanish America, was soon scattered far and wide, and disappeared for ever; but it is probable that only a small proportion of it fell into the hands of the liberators; for the new executive was not sufficiently well organised to carry out fully the decrees of confiscation. I do not think that the property to the value of six million sterling which was carried away by the Spanish garrison has been all traced, but the records of the day show that the Spaniards took every opportunity of escaping to sea in any sort of vessel they could procure, carrying with them all the property they could collect, in the hope of reaching the mother country or some neutral port.

It must have been a glorious time for adventurous persons not overburdened with scruples; for it seems that all the gold and precious stones of Peru were travelling about recklessly by sea and land without any proper protection. The pirates who then swarmed in those seas were not slow to avail themselves of this rare opportunity, and carried on a flourishing business until such time as they were caught and hanged by that terrible English admiral.

Numbers of piratical craft hovered around the Peruvian ports, and the badly equipped vessels of the Spanish fugitives fell an easy prey to them. But Lord Dundonald, on the other hand, was ever pursuing the pirates with great energy. He captured many of them, and, later on, he was able to boast that he had swept the West Coast clean of these scourges of the sea.

It is known, however, that several of these vessels escaped his vigilance, and that enormous quantities of cathedral plate and specie were never recovered from their hands.

The pirate vessel that succeeded in reaching the islet of Trinidad is supposed to have been one of these.

Captain P——, on leaving Bombay after the death of his quartermaster, had intended to land on Trinidad and examine the spot indicated on the pirate's plan; but as he had a rather unruly crew, and was himself crippled with a broken arm, he thought it prudent not to make the attempt then, and so passed the islet and sailed home.

On his return to England he told the pirate's story to many people, but of course preserved the secret of the exact position of the hiding-place. Nothing, however, seems to have been done towards recovering the treasure until 1880, when Captain P—— persuaded a shipping firm at Newcastle to allow one of their vessels trading to the Brazils to visit the island. It was arranged that the barquentine "John" should call at Trinidad on her way from Santos to Bull River, and that Captain P——'s son should go with the vessel so as to identify the spot and act on his father's behalf.

The "John" reached the islet, but, after beating about off it for a week, no landing-place could be found, and the captain decided to give up the attempt. But young P—— was very disinclined to return without having effected a landing, and persuaded the captain to allow him to swim ashore from a boat. The ship's long-boat was therefore put out, and was pulled as closely to the long roll of furious breakers as was considered safe. Then young P—— plunged into the sea, and contrived, after a narrow escape from drowning, to reach the land. The surf became more furious while he was on shore, so that it was impossible for him to swim off again that day. He had, consequently, to pass the night on the sands without either clothes or provisions, and was, moreover, in danger of being eaten alive by the land-crabs.

On the following morning the captain succeeded in casting the end of a line on shore, and the young man was dragged through the surf to the long-boat, and carried on board the vessel. He reported to the captain that he had discovered the spot described by the pirate; but that a great landslip of red débris had fallen on the treasure, which could not be removed without great labour. He said the place tallied exactly with the description furnished by his father, and that he firmly believed the story to be true and that the treasure was still there; but that he would not spend such another night on the island even if he could get the whole treasure for himself by doing so.

The captain of the "John," on hearing the young man's story, considered that any further attempt to land would involve great danger, which he would not be justified in risking, and, declining to lend further assistance in the matter, set sail at once for his destination.

The next expedition was organised by my informant, Mr. A—— of South Shields. The "Aurea," a barque of 600 tons burthen, was chartered. She was provided with lifeboats suitable for surf work, and an ample supply of picks, shovels, timber, blasting powder, and other stores. She was partly ballasted with a cargo of steam coal, which it was intended to sell in some foreign port, so as to pay part of the expenses of the expedition. The necessary funds were subscribed by several gentlemen, most of whom, I believe, accompanied the expedition. Proper agreements were drawn up, and were signed by the officers and members of the expedition, setting forth the proportion of the treasure each was to receive, should the search be successful.

This party also found the island to be almost inaccessible, on account of the surrounding circle of savage breakers, and experienced great difficulty in landing.

The following extract from the letter of one of the expedition describes only the commencement of their perils and adventures:—

"We sighted the island on March 23, 1885, but, as it was very squally weather, we could do nothing until the next morning, when we got out the lifeboat, fitted her with mast and sail, and loaded her with provisions and baggage. The ship towed us as near to the shore as was deemed prudent, and then left us to make the best of our way there, while she stood on her course. The weather was very wet and squally, and, with our deeply-laden boat, we found we made no progress, either with the sails or oars, and, after toiling until after sunset, we found ourselves in a most deplorable position. We were all wet to the skin, and exhausted with pulling, and the seas were continually on the point of swamping our boat. Darkness then set in; our vessel was out of sight, and we scarcely knew what to do. However, I took a lantern from among the stores, and got one of the men to light it and hoist it at our boat's masthead as a signal to our vessel. It blew out almost as soon as it was up, but we succeeded at last in sighting the vessel's port light, and got safely on board. The next day we determined to take the ship's boat and small dinghy with us, and tow the lifeboat ashore. We started early in the morning, the ship towing the three boats as close as possible to the Sugarloaf, and as the weather was now fine we soon got into South-west Bay, but found that the surf was much worse than we anticipated. We anchored the lifeboat with her cargo of stores close to the edge of the surf, and then Mr. D——, the mate, myself, and two hands, pulled along the weather side of the island, seeking a landing-place; but found a heavy surf at all points, and the bottom sown with sunken rocks. We then pulled back to South-west Bay, to consult with the others as to the best course to pursue. At last the mate volunteered to scull the dinghy ashore through the surf, if one man would go with him. One of the crew agreed to go, so they partly undressed, and took their places in the dinghy. A line was made fast to the stern, and as they pulled towards the shore we paid out, intending to haul the dinghy back again when they had reached the shore. All went well for a time, but when near the beach a tremendous roller caught the stern of the dinghy, drove the bow under, and turned her right over. The two men managed to get clear of the boat, and with some difficulty swam ashore."

Eventually Mr. A—— and seven other men succeeded in landing, carrying with them a limited quantity of provisions and some of the tools. They remained on the island from March 25 to April 17, during which time the vessel had been blown out of sight. Insufficient food and exposure to rain dispirited the men, and their imaginations were dismayed by the dismal aspect of these barren volcanic crags, and by the loathsome appearance of the land-crabs, which swarmed everywhere and continually attacked them.

They found what they considered to be the spot described by the pirate, but do not appear to have been quite so certain on this point as was young P——. Very little digging was actually done, "for," says Mr. A——, "we had few hands on shore capable of standing the heavy work under such a burning sun." They had only dug a small trench four feet deep into the landslip when the "Aurea" was sighted; then the sick and disheartened band refused to stay any longer on this accursed island, and insisted on being taken on board. So, leaving all their tools behind them—for in their anxiety to get away safely they would not be burdened with these—they were carried off to the vessel, so emaciated, weak, and ill that the captain came to the conclusion that he would lose most of his men if he landed them on so uninhabitable a spot, and, abandoning the search, he set sail for the West Indies.

This expedition, therefore, practically accomplished nothing. The problem as to whether the treasure was or was not lying under the landslips in South-west Bay was as far from solution as ever.

Before the departure of the "Aurea" expedition from South Shields, a good deal had been written concerning it in the English papers, with the result that some other adventurous spirits, having had their attention drawn to this possible El Dorado, hurried away to Trinidad in order to anticipate the Tynesiders. The following letter appeared in an English paper on May 14, 1885. The "Aurea" people, of course, knew nothing of this rival expedition, until they returned to England:—

TRINIDAD IN THE SOUTH ATLANTIC.

The Hidden Treasure Expedition.

[FROM A CORRESPONDENT.]

Kiel, May 11, 1885.

"Under this heading I have just now noticed a paragraph sent to the editor of a Danish daily paper, which, in its bearing on the well-known search-for-treasure expedition, may prove of interest to your readers, being in the shape of a letter sent from New York:—

"New York, April 17, 1885.

"On my arrival in New York from Aracaju, I read in your paper of January 14, 1885, about an expedition to be started from Newcastle, to proceed to the island of Trinidad in the South Atlantic, with the object in view of finding a treasure buried there some time ago by pirates; and I am in a position to furnish some particulars which, in all probability, are connected with this affair. On January 13, 1885, I was chartered with my vessel in Rio de Janeiro to take over to the above-mentioned island an American captain and four Portuguese sailors, together with a number of pickaxes, spades, &c., and a whale-boat. I was told that these people intended to go to this island to investigate if any 'guano' was to be found. A voyage of eleven days brought us there, but we had to keep off the shore on account of breakers for over three days. The men were then put ashore, and remained on the island for four days, during which time they were occupied with boring and digging, whereupon we sailed back to Bahia, and landed them there. I believe that these men, either by telegram from England or by other means, had heard of the existence of a treasure on this island, and that they meant to anticipate the English expedition. However, they found nothing. I noticed very well that the American captain, as well as his men, were highly disappointed. Let me take this opportunity to dissuade all masters of vessels to search in this uninhabited island for fresh water. It is a matter of great difficulty and danger to put boats on shore, through coral reefs. The indications on the charts for casting the lead should be a good deal further from the shore. During the time we were there the wind was N.N.E., and the current to S.W., upon a speed of from 12 to 15 quarter-miles in 24 hours. In South-west Bay, two cable-lengths from the shore, there is a reef not mentioned on the charts.

"H. N. ANKERSEN.
"Master of sailing vessel from Fanoe."

12

I found that the correspondent who sent this letter was correct in his information. When I called at Bahia with the "Alerte," my ship-chandler, Mr. Wilson, told me the whole of this story as it was related to him by the American adventurer on his arrival at Bahia from Trinidad. It is somewhat strange that the excavations made by this party were not seen by the "Aurea" people, who landed on the island within two months of the departure of the Americans; but this islet has been so shaken to its foundations by earthquake shock and volcanic action, that it is brittle from its mountain tops to the beach, and is in a state of perpetual change. Gigantic landslips are frequent, and I should not be surprised to find that all traces of our three months' hard digging have by now been entirely obliterated.

There might have been some fun, by the way, had the "Aurea" and the American arrived off the island at the same time.

Since my return, I have heard of two other expeditions which started from the other side of the Atlantic in search of the hidden treasure of Trinidad but, as with the former expeditions, nothing was accomplished. The loss of men and boats in the surf, sickness, and the numerous difficulties and dangers encountered, disheartened the men, and the attempt was abandoned before any serious work was done. It would seem as if this was one of those forlorn islands of which one reads in the old romances of the sea, on which the bloody deeds of the pirates have left a curse behind, so that the treasure is protected by evil spirits; and the great roaring seas which roll up seemingly without any natural cause, even after days of windless weather, and the ever-tottering crags, and all the forces and terrors of nature are made to keep man off from the inviolate hoard; while the loathsome land-crabs might well be the restless spirits of the pirates themselves, for they are indeed more ugly and evil, and generally more diabolical-looking, than the bloodiest pirate who ever lived.

CHAPTER II

THE "ALERTE" IS FITTED OUT

SUCH is the story of the Trinidad treasure, a story that seemed to me to bear the stamp of truth, and it was difficult to conceive that—allowing Captain P——'s narrative to be correct, and there is every reason to believe it as such—so many coincidences could have collected round a mere fabrication.

It is highly improbable that the foreign quartermaster evolved the whole matter from an imaginative brain, especially on his death-bed, when he was professing to confide a valuable secret to a friend as a token of his gratitude; neither can his statements be considered as being the ravings of a sick man, for they were far too circumstantial and compatible with facts.

In the first place, his carefully prepared plan of the island, the minute directions he gave as to the best landing, and his description of the features of the bay on whose shores the treasure was concealed, prove beyond doubt to myself and others who know Trinidad that he, or if not himself some informant of his, had landed on this so rarely visited islet; and not only landed, but passed some time on it, and carefully surveyed the approaches to the bay, so as to be able to point out the dangers and show the safest passage through the reefs. This information could not have been obtained from any pilot-book. The landing recommended by previous visitors is at the other side of the island. This bay is described by them as inaccessible, and the indications on the Admiralty chart are completely erroneous.

And, beyond this, the quartermaster must have been acquainted with what was taking place in two other distant portions of the world during the year of his professed landing on the desert island. He knew of the escape of pirates with the cathedral plate of Lima. He was also aware that, shortly afterwards, there were hanged in Cuba the crew of a vessel that had committed acts of piracy on the Peruvian coast. It is scarcely credible that an ordinary seaman—even allowing that he was superior in education to the average of his fellows —could have pieced these facts together so ingeniously into this plausible story.

It is needless to say that one like myself—who knew Trinidad, and who had personally sifted the evidence, and was constantly coming across numbers of incidents not mentioned here, trifling in themselves, but, taken together, strongly corroborative—would be more impressed by the coincidences, and consequently be more inclined to give credence to the story than one who merely reads the narrative in the pages of this book.

Hence the result of my interview with Mr. A—— was that I decided to sail to Trinidad and search for the treasure. I knew, of course, that the chances were greatly against my finding anything. I was quite prepared for complete failure; but I considered that there was a sufficient possibility of success to make the venture worth the undertaking.

I, of course, saw that the great impediment was the landslip, which might have covered the landmarks, and so altered the features of the ravine as to render recognition of the exact spot extremely difficult; for it is quite possible that young Mr. P—— was somewhat over-sanguine and that the grounds for his so readily identifying the pirate's hiding-place were inadequate.

The former adventurers seem to have considered that the difficulties of landing constituted almost as great an obstacle to success as the landslip itself; but I was confident that these difficulties were anything but insuperable and that, by taking proper precautions, it would be quite possible to land a working party with all necessary stores and tools, and even, if necessary, heavy machinery as well. I had myself, nine years previously, landed at three different points of the island, and had passed several days on shore, so I quite realised what was before me.

There is no doubt that the former adventurers failed from precipitancy. Patience is a necessary quality for those who wish to land on Trinidad. One must not expect to sail there and forthwith disembark with one's baggage as if it were on Southsea Pier. It appears, too, that the captains of the square-rigged vessels which carried the expeditions to the island were largely responsible for the failure of the former quests; they would not approach the islands within several miles; they became anxious as to the safety of their boats and men, were fidgety to sail away again to the safety of the broad ocean, and hurried the adventurers off the shore before they had had scarce time to look around them. The captains, no doubt, were quite right from their point of view; but it is also certain that the treasure could never be recovered by this way of going to work. To dig away the landslip would involve many months of labour, and during that time the captain of the vessel must be prepared to stand off and on, or heave-to off the island—for to remain at anchor for any length of time would be dangerous. And again, there must be no hurry in landing: the working party may have to remain on board the vessel for weeks at a stretch gazing at that wild shore, before it be possible for them to attain it. I have seen the great rollers dashing on the beach with a dreadful roar for days together, and the surf—as the "South Atlantic Directory" observes without any exaggeration—"is often incredibly great, and has been seen to break over a bluff which is two hundred feet high."

Notwithstanding this, if one is patient and bides one's opportunity, there are days when landing can be accomplished without any difficulty whatever.

When I visited Trinidad with the "Falcon" I discovered one especially safe landing-place on the lee side of the island, where a natural pier of coral projects into the sea beyond the breakers. I knew that it was possible to effect a landing here ten times to once that this could be done on the more exposed beach of the bay under the Sugarloaf, where the "Aurea" party landed. A considerable and, I believe, perennial stream of water runs down as a cascade into the sea close to my landing-place, and I knew that it would be easy to disembark here a quantity of provisions, and establish a depot to which the working party in Sugarloaf Bay could repair in the case of their stores falling short and their communication with the vessel being cut off by bad weather. I had myself crossed the lofty mountains which separate this landing-place from the bay under the Sugarloaf, and knew that, though difficult, they were not inaccessible.

My negotiations with Mr. A—— terminated in his furnishing me with the bearings of the hidden treasure, and handing over to me the copy of the pirate's plan of the island, which the "Aurea" people had taken with them. This plan merely indicated the safest landing-place in the bay.

Mr. A——'s account of his own experiences were of great service to me in fitting out this expedition. He told me that there was no constant stream of fresh water on the shores of this bay, or anywhere near it; but that a little water of an inferior quality could be collected after rain. There was, however, according to him, an abundance of dead wood on the hill-sides, which served admirably as fuel; so I took note that a condensing apparatus would be an indispensable addition to our stores. He told me that I should find the "Aurea" tools lying on the beach, which, if not too corroded, might be of use to us. We did eventually find some of these, and employed them in our operations: I have now in my possession an "Aurea" pick which I brought away with me. I have to thank Mr. A—— for a variety of valuable hints, which I did not neglect.

Having decided to go, the first thing to be done was to find a vessel, a fore-and-after which could accommodate thirteen or fourteen men on an ocean voyage, and which would yet be easily handled by two or three while hove-to off the island.

I went down to my old head-quarters, Southampton, and explained what I was in search of to Mr. Picket, of West Quay, who had been my shipwright from my earliest yachting days, and who fitted out the old "Falcon" for her long voyage. With his assistance I soon discovered a very suitable vessel, the cutter-yacht "Alerte," of fifty-six tons yacht measurement, and thirty-three tons register. This was, therefore, a considerably larger vessel than the "Falcon," with which I had made my first voyage to Trinidad, for she was twenty-four feet shorter than the "Alerte," and was only of fifteen tons register.

The dimensions of the "Alerte" are as follows:—length, 64·3 feet; beam 14·5 feet; depth, 9 feet. She was built by Ratsey of Cowes in 1864, so she is rather an ancient vessel; but she was constructed, in a much stronger fashion than is usual in these days, of thoroughly seasoned teak. There had been no scamping of work in her case, and now, after twenty-six years of service, she is as sound as on the day she left the stocks; there is not a weak spot in her, and she is in fact a far more reliable craft than a newer vessel would have proved; for, even as a human life is more secure after it has safely passed through the period of infantile disorders, so a vessel, if she does not develop dry-rot within a few years of her launching, is not likely to do so afterwards. She has proved herself to have been honestly put together of seasoned timber, and not of sappy rubbish.

The "Alerte," moreover, was of the good old-fashioned build, with ample beam, and not of the modern plank-on-end style. She had only two tons of lead outside, the remainder of her ballast was in her hold—a great advantage for real cruising; for a vessel with a lead mine on her keel cannot but strain herself in heavy weather with the violent jerkiness of her action, instead of rolling about with a leisurely motion on the top of the water as if she were quite at home there, like a vessel of the comfortable "Alerte" type.

This was not the first ocean cruise the gallant old cutter had undertaken; for she once accomplished the voyage from Southampton to Sydney in 103 days, which is very creditable work.

She was provided, I found, with new sails by Lapthorn, and an excellent inventory throughout, so little was required besides making the alterations necessary for the particular objects of our cruise. I accordingly purchased the vessel, very pleased at having without delay discovered a craft so suitable, and put her into Mr. Picket's hands to be got ready for sea. While this was being done I let it be widely known that I was organising a treasure-hunting expedition and was in search of volunteers. Numbers applied, and I gradually selected my crew, some of whom made themselves of use in assisting me to fit out at Southampton.

A cruise of this description involves a good deal of preparation. In the first place, seeing that the "Alerte" was a somewhat heavily sparred vessel, I resolved to convert her into a yawl. So the main boom and gaff were shortened, the area of the mainsail considerably reduced, and a mizen mast was stepped in the counter, on which we set a snug jib-headed sail. No other alterations of importance were required on deck.

Below we had to find room for, and construct, extra bunks, and extra water-tanks occupied all available room. A condensing apparatus intended for use on the island was made for me by Mr. Hornsey of Southampton. The boiler was a strong twenty-gallon drum, and a forty-gallon tank contained the worm. At sea these two were disconnected and lashed in the saloon, serving as water tanks. We carried in all 600 gallons of water. The precious fluid was, of course, never used for washing purposes at sea. Salt-water-soap and the Atlantic had to content us for our ablutions, and, where possible, seawater was employed for cooking purposes as well.

The "Alerte" carried two boats, a dinghy and a gig. We condemned the gig, as being quite unfit for our work, and left her behind. As a capacious lifeboat was necessary for landing men and stores on the island, Mr. White of Cowes built one for us—a light yet strong mahogany boat, double ended, with water-tight compartments at either end. She was easy to pull, considering her size, and sailed fairly well under two sprit-sails. We carried this boat on deck on the starboard side, as she was too heavy for our davits. The dinghy, on the other hand, was always swung on the port davits.

As the stores would put down the vessel a good deal, we took out of her a corresponding weight of ballast—about eight tons. Two tiers of lead were removed from under the saloon floor, and in the space thus gained we stowed the greater part of our tools.

Among these was a complete set of boring apparatus constructed for us by Messrs. Tilley, by means of which we should be enabled to explore through earth and rock to the depth of fifty feet We also carried a Tangye's hydraulic jack, capable of lifting twelve tons, which we found of service when large rocks had to be removed from the trenches. Shovels, picks, crow-bars, iron wheelbarrows, carpenters' and other tools; a port-able forge and anvil, dogs and other materials for timbering a shaft if necessary, and a variety of other useful implements were on board. We took with us two of Messrs. Piggot's large emigrant tents, wire-fencing with which to surround our camp and so keep off the land-crabs, a few gardener's tools and seeds of quick-growing vegetables for the kitchen-garden which we intended to plant on the island—a horticultural scheme which never came off in consequence of the want of water—taxidermic gear with view to the rare sea-birds that breed on the island, medical stores and surgical instruments, fishing-tackle; and, in short, we were well-equipped with all needful things, a full inventory of which would nearly fill this book.

Neither did we omit the precaution of arming ourselves in case any one should choose to molest us, a not altogether im-probable event; for there was a talk of rival expeditions start-ing for the island at the very time we were fitting out; our plans had been fully discussed in the newspapers, despite our attempt to keep secret our destination at least; and I called to mind the Yankee vessel that had endeavoured to anticipate the "Aurea." Should some such vessel appear on the scene just as we had come across the treasure, it would be well for us to be prepared to defend it.

Each man, therefore, was provided with a Colt's repeating-rifle, and in addition to these there were other rifles and several revolvers on board, and no lack of ammunition for every weapon. The Duke of Sutherland kindly lent us one of Bland's double-barrelled whaling-guns, which was carried on his Grace's yacht, the "Sans Peur," during her foreign cruises. This was a quick-firing and formidable weapon, discharging steel shot, grape, shell, and harpoons, and capable of sending to the bottom any wooden vessel. I think the sight of it inspired some of my crew with ideas almost piratical. I have heard them express the opinion that it was a shame to have such a gun lying idle on board, and that an opportunity ought to be found of testing its powers.

Of the provisioning of the "Alerte" I need say little, for all foreign-going vessels are provisioned more or less in the same way; but to foresee all that would be necessary for thirteen men for a period of at least six months, and to stow away this great bulk of stores, was not the least troublesome part of our fitting out.

Former experience had taught me that it would not do to rely too much on tinned meats, more especially in the tropics. I am confident that a diet composed principally of these is extremely unwholesome, and to this cause alone can be attributed an illness that attacked the whole crew of the "Falcon" during the latter months of her South American voyage. The old-fashioned sea-food is the best after all. Salt beef and salt pork, even after it has travelled a few times round the world, and is consequently somewhat malodorous, forms a far more sustaining diet than the very best of tinned meats. The instinct of the sailor teaches him this; as a rule he detests the flabby, overcooked stuff out of the cans, and, even if he tolerates it, will always prefer to it the commonest mess beef, which in odour, taste, and appearance would be horrible to a fastidious person. But let this same person have been at sea for a few months, and the chances are that he will look forward with pleasure to the days on which the salt junk appears on the ship's bill of fare.

So, though we took on board a large quantity of tinned meats of various kinds, we also had some 600 pounds of beef and pork salted down for us, with which we filled the vessel's harness casks and meat tanks. This meat was of the very best quality, and for this very reason a great deal of it was spoiled and had to be thrown overboard. It had been salted too recently. Barrels of ancient mess beef soaked with saltpetre and hardened into almost the consistency of a deal board, though far from being so tasty as was our meat before it was tainted, would have answered our purpose far better, and would have kept well despite the high temperature of a small vessel in the tropics.

In the same way a short-sighted love of luxury induced us to supply the vessel with barrels of the best cabin biscuit. The result was that our bread, long before the termination of the cruise, was swarming with maggots and an exceedingly unpleasant species of small beetle, and was, in addition to this, attacked by mildew. A commoner quality of ship's bread would not have spoiled so readily, for it is known that insects thrive best and multiply amazingly on this tempting first-class flour.

All sorts of preserved food, jams, vegetables, &c., were of course included in our store-list, as was also the indispensable lime-juice—the vessel was, in short, supplied with a sufficient quantity of necessaries and luxuries.

We got our tobacco out of bond, also our rum, which was the only alcoholic beverage on board; it certainly is the most wholesome spirit for sea use, especially within the tropics.

During the first portion of the voyage small rations of rum were served out daily to each person on board. Later on, when it was clear that none of the gentlemen-adventurers showed any inclination to exceed in this respect at sea, the first mate, Mr. Meredyth, petitioned me to give up the ration system so far as they were concerned, and to allow the bottle of spirit to be put on the saloon table at dinner for their free use. This was done, with no bad result. The paid hands were, of course, always limited to rations of spirit.

CHAPTER III

THE SHIP'S COMPANY

To fit out and store a vessel for a lengthy expedition may be a somewhat arduous task, but it is an interesting and pleasant one, which is more than can be said with regard to that equally important work, the choice of one's companions. One cannot make any very serious mistake in the selection of one's provisions, but to take the wrong man with one on a voyage that involves a complete severance from all the influences of civilisation for months at a time may bring exceedingly unpleasant consequences.

I determined to ship as few paid hands as possible, and to outnumber them with a chosen body of what, in the parlance of the old privateering days, may be termed gentlemen-adventurers, volunteers who would contribute to the cost of the expedition, would work as sailors on board and as navvies on the island, and who would each be entitled to receive a considerable share of the proceeds of the venture should anything be discovered. The officers of the vessel would be selected from this body and I myself would act as captain. In this way the causes which led to the failure of some of the previous expeditions would be wanting. The professional sailors would be unable—in their disinclination to face the difficulties of the island—to insist on the adventurers abandoning the project. There would be no paid captain to lay down the law to his employers.

I knew that by the time we should reach Trinidad even those gentlemen who had never been to sea before would have learnt a good deal, so that in the case of our paid hands proving mutinous we could dispense with them altogether. I was well aware that if I undertook such an expedition with a paid crew of the ordinary type, far outnumbering the gentlemen aft, the value of the treasure, if discovered, would not improbably tempt them to murder their officers and employers

THE CRUISE OF THE ALERTE

and seize it for themselves. With a majority of volunteers on board, each entitled to a large share in the find, all risk of this description would be avoided.

I decided that our complement should be thirteen all told, consisting of nine gentlemen-adventurers, myself included, and four paid hands.

The following are extracts from some of the clauses of the agreement which was entered into between myself and the volunteers:—

"Mr. E. F. Knight undertakes to provide a vessel, stores, &c., suitable for the expedition, and to provide at least sufficient provisions for the voyage out and home and six months besides.

"Each member of the expedition will pay in advance to Mr. Knight 100*l.*, and undertake to work both on board and on shore under Mr. Knight's directions. This 100*l.* will be the extent of each member's liability.

"During the first six months from the time of landing on the island, the enterprise can only be abandoned with the consent of Mr. Knight, and on decision by vote of three-quarters of the members. After six months have elapsed, a majority of three-quarters of the members will determine whether the enterprise is to be continued or abandoned.

"Each member, or, if he die in the course of the expedition, his legal representative, will receive one-twentieth of the gross proceeds of the venture.

"If any member of the expedition mutiny or incite to mutiny, he shall be tried by a court-martial of the other members of the expedition, and, if it be decided by a majority of three-quarters that the offence be sufficiently grave, he shall forfeit all share in the proceeds of the expedition, subject to an appeal to the English Courts on his return.

"None of these rules apply to the paid hands on the vessel."

The paid hands received good wages and were entitled to no share of the treasure, though they, of course, knew well that, should our search prove successful and their conduct have been satisfactory, they would receive a substantial present.

It would, of course, have been very pleasant for me to have selected my volunteers from among my own friends, especially those who had been at sea with me before; but this I found to be impossible, at any rate at such short notice. I knew dozens of men who would have liked nothing better than to have joined me, but all were engaged in some profession or other which it would have been folly to have neglected for so problematic a gain. The type of man who is willing to toil hard, endure discomfort and peril, and abandon every luxury for nine months on the remote chance of discovering treasure, and is, moreover, willing to pay 100*l.* for the privileges of doing so, is not to be found easily, either in the professional or wealthy classes.

There are, doubtless, thousands of Englishmen willing to embark on a venture of this description, but it is obvious that there is a likelihood of a fair percentage of these volunteers being adventurers in the unfavourable sense of the term—men anxious to get away from England for reasons not creditable to themselves, men too, of the rolling-stone description and more or less worthless in a variety of ways, and who would be more likely than the paid sailors to wax discontented and foment mutiny. I realised that the selection of my men should be made with great care.

Of volunteers I had no lack. An article in the *St. James's Gazette* describing my project brought me applications to join from something like 150 men.

Some of the letters I received were great curiosities in their way, and would cause much amusement could I publish them. I interviewed some sixty of the applicants, and this was certainly far the most arduous and difficult work connected with the undertaking, so far as I was concerned. I shall never forget how weary I became of the repetition to each fresh visitor of the conditions and object of the voyage, and with what dread I looked forward to my visits to the little club at which these interviews were held.

All manner of men made appointments to meet me—the sanguine young spirits eager for adventure, the cautious and suspicious who would not risk their 100*l.* unless they were guaranteed a return of 50,000*l.* or so. There were also those who wasted my time out of mere curiosity, never having entertained any intention of joining me, and others who hoped to pump enough information out of me to enable them to earn a few guineas by writing an article for the newspapers.

But the majority of my applicants were in earnest, and I will here take the opportunity of expressing my regret if, in the midst of all the hurry and worry of that time, I omitted to reply to some of my correspondents. All the preparations for the voyage had to be carried out in a very limited space of time, in order that we should get away from England before the autumnal equinox; I was fitting out the vessel and selecting gentlemen-adventurers simultaneously, constantly travelling backwards and forwards between London and Southampton, and by the time we were ready for sea I was pretty well worn out with anxious work.

One by one I selected my men, and those who saw them congratulated me on having got together a most promising-looking crew. Some, it is true, proved themselves to be quite unsuitable for the purpose; but at the end of the expedition, when we were at Port of Spain, I had on board seven men at least who were ready to go anywhere and do anything with me, all of them more cheerful, fit and capable in every respect than they were on leaving Southampton.

References were brought to me by each volunteer for the expedition. I know how worthless references generally are, but never before did I so strongly realise this fact. The most undesirable person can often produce excellent testimonials from undoubtedly worthy people, who have met him in London society, for instance, but who know absolutely nothing of the true nature of the man, least of all of how he would prove himself in such an undertaking as this was, when traits are revealed that do not generally declare themselves in a drawing-room.

The volunteer whom I made first mate turned out very badly. He was afraid himself, and he did his best to scare the other gentlemen and the paid hands. He came to the conclusion that the "Alerte" was a bad sea-boat, cranky, too heavily sparred, and generally too small and unsafe to be entrusted with his valuable life. I found out afterwards that a little conspiracy was hatching to compel me to sell the "Alerte" in the Cape Verde Islands for what she would fetch, and charter a large Yankee schooner. He endeavoured to disseminate discontent behind my back and to undermine my authority, with the sole result that he made himself detestable to his companions fore and aft, and ultimately, having made the vessel too warm to hold him, packed up his traps and deserted her at Bahia without giving me any reason for so doing.

Not content to desert himself, he did his best to persuade others to do likewise. He succeeded with one timid individual, who also went off at Bahia—luckily, for us, as we did not want him. There was yet a third who had half a mind to desert with them, but who remained with us, a discontented young man to the end. Being the one man of the sort left on board, his opinions were a matter of indifference to us; but he was the sole cause of those "disagreements" of which he has since complained in print, and I have no doubt made his own life "disagreeable" enough. To do him justice, he was the ablest swimmer and the best judge of blue china on board.

I should not have alluded to our squabbles in this book had not the men who caused them spread all manner of false reports on their return, which have appeared in the newspapers and magazines. Therefore, instead of treating the whole matter with the contempt it deserves, I am justified, I think, in entering into this explanation on behalf of myself and of my loyal companions who stuck to the expedition to the end.

Only one other of my companions aft voluntarily left me, a very good fellow, who had undertaken a job the nature of which he had not fully realised; for the sea, at any rate as viewed from a yacht, had such terrors for him, and his health suffered to such an extent, that, under our doctor's advice, he left us at St. Vincent. I believe that a good deal of his nervousness was due to the insinuations of the first mate's evil tongue.

Having rid ourselves of these two people at Bahia, everything went on much better, all work was done more promptly and smoothly, the old friction disappeared, a cloud seemed to have been lifted from the vessel, cheerfulness prevailed, and when we sailed to Trinidad and the real business and difficulties commenced all was got through in a most satisfactory fashion.

Grumbling is the Englishman's privilege on land, still more so at sea, where some growling is absolutely necessary to relieve the monotony of ship-life; after leaving Bahia an unusually small amount of this privilege was enjoyed on the "Alerte."

As I was taking a fair number of paid hands with me, I did not consider it necessary that all the gentlemen-adventurers should have a knowledge of seamanship. Indeed, I believe that only the first mate and the doctor had ever before handled a fore-and-after. However, most of the others were willing, and soon learnt to take a trick at the tiller and haul at a rope in a satisfactory manner.

Some of the volunteers did not treat me quite fairly, for, after deciding to join me and so causing me to refuse other eligible candidates, they discovered at the very last moment that something prevented them from going. This naturally put me to great inconvenience, and obliged me to take others, to replace them, at the shortest notice. Thus I had to ship my last two men the day before we sailed.

Remembering how interesting was the scenery of Trinidad, I had intended to acquire some knowledge of photography and carry an apparatus with me. But one of my volunteers professed to be an excellent amateur photographer, and as he promised to take upon himself that part of the work I relied upon him to do so and left it to him. He was one of those who failed to turn up on the day of sailing, and we had to put to sea, to my great regret afterwards, without a camera.

We were equally unfortunate with our taxidermist. One of the volunteers had undertaken to take lessons in bird-skinning at my suggestion; for I knew that Trinidad was the principal breeding-place for sea-birds in the South Atlantic, and that very rare specimens can be collected there. He, too, never reached the desert island—more, I must allow, on account of illness than through any fault of his own. But it was very disappointing, for all that.

For such a voyage as the one contemplated the presence of a surgeon was advisable. A young doctor was therefore included among the gentlemen-adventurers—Mr. Cloete Smith, who also occupied the post of mate after the desertion of the officers at Bahia.

Of the four paid hands one, the boatswain, only accompanied us as far as Teneriffe.

Our cook, John Wright, had been with me on three previous voyages as sole hand. One of our A. B.'s was Arthur Cotton, who, as a boy nine years before, had been the only paid hand on the "Falcon" when we sailed from Southampton to South America. In the course of that voyage he had visited Trinidad with me, and was now able to spin to his shipmates long and more or less fantastic yarns concerning the place we were bound to. The strange island had evidently made a great impression on his imagination. Our other A. B. was Ted Milner, a lad from the North Sea fishing-smacks.

CHAPTER IV

A ROMANCE OF THE SALVAGES

THE article in the *St. James's Gazette* attracted a considerable amount of attention, as was proved by the bewildering mass of correspondence with reference to the expedition which I received during the weeks preceding our departure. Many of these letters were prompted evidently by mere curiosity, others contained suggestions—of which some were sensible enough; a few, whimsical in the extreme. Cranks wrote to me who professed to be acquainted with certain methods for discovering treasure by means of divining rods, or charms, or other uncanny tricks. Others had dreamt dreams, in which they had seen the exact position of the wealth; but, most curious of all were the letters from individuals in all parts of Europe and America who were acquainted with the existence of other treasures, which they proposed I should search for in the course of my voyage. To have sought them all would have meant to sail every navigable sea on the face of the earth, and to have travelled into the heart of continents; in short, to have undertaken a voyage which would have extended over a century or so. To have found them all would have necessitated my chartering all the merchant fleets of Europe to carry them home; and then gold would have become a valueless drug on the markets, and my labours would have been all in vain.

One individual modestly asked for 1,000*l.* down before he would give the slightest hint as to the nature of his treasure or its locality; but, according to him, there could not be the slightest doubt as to my finding it, and as one item alone of this pile consisted of ten million pounds worth of golden bars, it would be the height of folly on my part not to send him a cheque for the comparatively ridiculous sum of 1,000*l.* in return for such information.

Some of these treasure-tales were very terrible, and the most bloodthirsty villains figured in the ghastly narratives. Among my correspondence I have materials that would supply all our writers of boys' stories for years.

But in addition to the numerous impossible tales, there were some well authenticated, and people who had taken an interest in these matters, and had carefully collected their data, wrote to me concerning several promising schemes.

A few days before sailing, a retired naval officer residing in Exeter came to see me at Southampton; he told me he had guessed that our destination was the islet of Trinidad, and that he was acquainted with the record of another treasure which had been concealed on a desert island lying on our route, distant about 1,400 miles from Southampton and 3,400 from Trinidad; and he thought it would be worth our while to make a call there, and endeavour to identify the spot.

An outline of this story is given in the "North Atlantic Directory," but the following account was copied by my informant from the Government documents relating to the matter.

Early in 1813 the then Secretary of the Admiralty wrote to Sir Richard Bickerton, the Commander-in-Chief at Portsmouth, instructing him to let a seaman who had given information respecting a hidden treasure be sent in the first King's ship likely to touch at Madeira, so that the truth of his story might be put to the test.

The "Prometheus," Captain Hercules Robinson, was then refitting at Portsmouth, and to this officer was entrusted the carrying out of the Admiralty orders. In his report Captain Robinson states that after being introduced to the foreign seaman referred to in the above letter, and reading the notes which had been taken of his information, he charged him to tell no person what he knew or what was his business, that he was to mess with the captain's coxswain, and that no duty would be required of him. To this the man replied that that was all he desired, that he was willing to give his time, and would ask no remuneration if nothing resulted from his intelligence.

A few days afterwards the ship sailed, and in a week

anchored at Funchal, Madeira. During the passage, Captain Robinson took occasion to examine and cross-question the man, whose name was Christian Cruise, and compare his verbal with his written testimony.

The substance of both was that some years before he was sent to the hospital in Santa Cruz, with yellow fever, with a Spanish sailor, who had served for three or four voyages in the Danish merchant ship in which Cruise was employed. He was in a raging fever, but, notwithstanding, recovered. The Spaniard, though less violently ill, sank under a gradual decay in which medical aid was unavailing, and, a few days before his death, told Cruise he had something to disclose which troubled him, and accordingly made the following statement.

He said that in 1804 he was returning in a Spanish ship from South America to Cadiz, with a cargo of produce and about two millions of dollars in chests, that when within a few days' sail of Cadiz they boarded a neutral, who told them that, their four galleons had been taken by a squadron of English frigates, war having been declared, and that a cordon of cruisers from Trafalgar to Cape Finisterre would make it impossible for any vessel to reach Cadiz, or any other Spanish port. What was to be done? Returning to South America was out of the question, and the captain resolved to try back for the West Indies, run for the north part of the Spanish Main or some neutral island, and have a chance thus of saving at least the treasure with which he was intrusted. The crew, who preferred the attempt of making Cadiz, were all but in a state of mutiny. But they acquiesced in the proceeding, and, keeping out of the probable track of cruisers, reached a few degrees to the southward of Madeira, where they hoped to meet the trade-winds.

They had familiarised their minds to plans of resistance and outrage, but had not the heart to carry them into effect, till, one daybreak, they found themselves off a cluster of small uninhabited islands fifty leagues to the southward of Madeira, and nearly in its longitude, the name of which the narrator did not know. The central island, about three miles round, was high, flat and green at top, but clearly uninhabited; the

temptation was irresistible: here was a place where everything might be hidden; why run risks to avoid the English, in
order to benefit their captain and the owners? why not serve
themselves? The captain was accordingly knocked on the
head, or stabbed and carried below, and the ship hauled in to
what appeared the anchorage on the south side of the island.
There they found a snug little bay, in which they brought up,
landed the chests of dollars, and cut a deep trench in the
white sand above high water mark, and buried the treasure
and covered it over, and, some feet above the chests, deposited
in a box the body of their murdered captain. They then put
to sea, resolving to keep well to the southward, and try to make
the Spanish Main or a neutral island, run the ship on shore and
set her on fire, agree on some plausible lie, and with the portion
of the money which they retained and carried on their persons
they were to purchase a small vessel, and, under English or
other safe colours, to revisit their hoard, and carry it off at
once or in portions. In time, they passed Tobago, and in their
clumsy, ignorant navigation, while it was blowing hard, ran
on an uninhabited cay on which the ship went to pieces, and
only two lives were saved. These got to Santa Cruz or St.
Thomas, one died, and the other was the seaman who made
the statement to Christian Cruise. The name of the ship, the
owners, the port she sailed from, the exact date, or various
other particulars by which the truth might be discovered, were
not told to Christian Cruise, or not remembered.

Captain Robinson gave at length and in a quaint old-
fashioned way his impressions as to the *bona fides* of Cruise.
He says:—"May he not have some interested object in fabri-
cating this story? Why did he not tell it before? Is not the
cold-blooded murder inconceivable barbarity, and the burying the body over the treasure too dramatic and buccaneer;
like? or might not the Spaniard have lied from love of lying
and mystifying his simple shipmate, or might he not have
been raving?" Captain Robinson then thus satisfactorily
replies to his own queries: "As to the first difficulty, I had the
strongest conviction of the honesty of Christian Cruise, and I
think I could hardly be grossly deceived as to his character,

33

and his disclaiming any reward unless the discovery was made went to confirm my belief that he was an honest man. And then, as to his withholding his information for four or five years, be it remembered that the war with Denmark might truly have shut him out from any possibility of intercourse with England. Next, as to the wantonness and indifference with which the murder was perpetrated: I am afraid there is no great improbability in this; with self-interest in the scales, humanity is but as dust in the balance. I have witnessed a disregard of human life in matters of promotion in our service, &c., even among men of gentle blood, which makes the conduct of these Spaniards under vehement temptation, and when they could do as they pleased, sufficiently intelligible. But, certainly, the coffin over the treasure looked somewhat theatrical, had given it the air of Sadler's Wells or a novel, rather than matter of fact. I enquired, therefore, from Christian why the body was thus buried, and he replied that he understood the object was, that in case any person should find the marks of their proceeding, and dig to discover what they had been about, they might come to the body and go no further. Then, as to the supposition of the Spaniard lying from mere *méchanceté*, this conduct would be utterly out of keeping in an ignorant Spanish seaman. But, lastly, he might have been raving, and on this point I was particular in my enquiries. Cruise said, "Certainly not, he was quite clear in his mind; his conscience might be troubled, but his head was not disturbed," and it is conceivable enough that this dying criminal might have been able to bring into such correct review, as he was stated to have done, these portions of his dark history. The result of my enquiries and cogitations on the subject was, that the probability was strongly in favour of the substantial truth of this romance of real life, that I considered would be still further substantiated if the *locus in quo*, the Salvages (for to them alone the latitude and longitude pointed), corresponded with the account given of the tomb of the dollars."

Captain Robinson goes on to state that he enquired at Madeira whether anything had ever been picked up at the

Salvages, and was informed that some years before the taffrail of a foreign ship had been found there and two boxes of dollars. Being unable to obtain any precise information, he then proceeded for the island. On arriving off the Great Salvage they found it was about a league in circumference, flat at top, and green with salsola and saltwort and other alcalescent plants; and on hauling round the east point opened up a sandy bay with white beach and the little level spot above high water mark just as they wanted to find it. Captain Robinson asked Christian, "Will this do?" and the man replied, "No doubt, sir, it must be the place." The captain then sent for the officers, and, pledging them to secrecy that others might not interfere with them, told them all the story, but desired them to announce only half the truth to the men—namely, that they were in search of a murdered man who was supposed to be buried somewhere above high water mark. Fifty or sixty of the ship's crew were then landed, provided with all the shovels there were on board, and boarding-pikes; and to encourage them they were told that the discoverer of the coffin should have a reward of one hundred dollars. Their embarrassment, however, was now extreme; the white sand extended round the bay, and a large area intervened between the high water and the foot of the cliff, which a month would not turn up. They selected the centre of the beach and went beyond high water mark to where Captain Robinson thought the breaking of the sea and the drainage through the sand might terminate, and where a man would be likely to drop his burden, and then they dug a deep hole, but with no greater success than finding some broken shells and rounded pebbles. The men in the meanwhile were probing with their boarding-pikes in all directions, and digging in every promising spot. This went on for several hours, and finally the captain abandoned the search and ordered the boats on board, and, as night was approaching and the ship's situation unsafe, hoisted them in, weighed, and stood out of the bay and shaped course for Madeira. On arriving at Funchal they found other orders and occupation, and had no opportunity of revisiting the spot before their return to England. Nor did the Admiralty of the day, on receiving Captain Robinson's report, think it worth while to prosecute the matter further.

In conclusion, Captain Robinson remarks that, "In favour of the affirmative view, there is the apparent honesty, fairness, candour, and clearheadedness of Christian Cruise, as well as the entire correspondence of the place with that described; and opposed to this are the many motives to falsehood, deceit, and self-interest in some obscure shape, or even mere love of lying; or it may be the ravings of lunacy and the wonderful plausibility of perverted reason. If I am asked for my own opinion, I would say that my judgment leans, as I have already declared, to the probability of some such transaction having taken place, so much so that I certainly think it worth the while of any yachtsman to try what this might turn up."

My informant from Exeter told me that he had sailed by these islands close in shore while he was serving in the navy, and he gave me an account of their appearance. He said he had perceived men on the Great Salvage, and understood that Portuguese or other fishermen visit the island at one season of the year in order to catch and salt down the fish that abound in the surrounding sea. He did not consider that there was ever a large body of these men on the island, so that in the event of our digging there and discovering the treasure, our party would be strong enough, well armed as we were, to protect and carry it off in spite of any opposition that might be offered.

As my informant pointed out, one curious feature in this vague and not very encouraging tale of hidden treasure was that the foreign seaman, according to the report, stated that the chests of dollars were landed on the middle island, whereas Captain Robinson prosecuted his search on the Great Salvage, or northern-most island.

The Salvages—see the chart—consist of three islands, of which the middle one, known as the Great Piton, is the largest; and if the man's tale be true, it is on this island that the treasure should be sought.

It would not be worth while to fit out an expedition to the Salvages on such evidence as this; "but," argued my inormant, "as you must pass near the group with your vessel, it would not delay you much to discover whether any bay answering to the man's description exists on the south side of the Great Piton."

I told this gentleman that I would put the matter before my companions, and that in case they agreed to this deviation from our original scheme we would, if possible, land on the Great Piton and explore the likely portions of the sands for the chests of dollars.

Seeing that the Salvages, adjacent as they are to both Madeira and the Canaries, might belong to either Spain or Portugal—though I could find no record of such being the case—I thought it prudent to keep this portion of our programme a secret; for the publication of our intentions in the papers might attract the attention of those who laid claim to the islets and cause them to interfere with our operations. Consequently, when we sailed only three men knew whither we were bound, and I said nothing about the Salvages until we had been two days at sea, when I repeated the whole story to my companions after dinner. They were unanimously of opinion that we should visit the island and see what could be done there. Our course was accordingly shaped for it. We talked over the possibility of finding foreign fishermen on the Salvages, and some of my companions proposed that in this case we should take charge of their boats for them during our stay, so that they would have no means of communicating with their countries and giving notice of our arrival. Having thus, as it were, taken temporary possession of the island, we were to compel the fishermen to dig for us at a reasonable rate of pay—a somewhat high-handed proceeding, but the suggestion at any rate showed that there were those among my crew who would not be deterred by small difficulties, when impelled by the prospect of discovering gold.

I was unable to take a bill of health for our first port of call, as I did not myself know what it would be, our stoppages on the way out entirely depending on our necessities, such as want of water or repairs of any damage to the vessel. If it had been possible to have done so I would have called at no inhabited place until the termination of the expedition; but I was well aware that the lack of something or other would sooner or later drive us into port. I accordingly procured a bill of health for Sydney; not that I had the slightest intention of going there, but I knew that this document would satisfy the authorities of any place at which I was likely to call for stores: every harbour on either side of the Atlantic can be considered as being more or less on the way to Australia, and on entering a port a visé of our bill of health would be all that was necessary; for there is no law against zigzagging across the world to one's destination in a leisurely fashion if one chooses to do so.

CHAPTER V

OUR FIRST VOYAGE

OUR preparations were hurried on at Southampton, and I was never left in peace, but was in a condition of perpetual work and travel, my sole relaxation being the frequent farewell dinners given to myself and my companions by our friends and sympathisers; and very jolly as these dinners were, they were relaxations in the other sense of the term rather than reposeful amusements for a weary man. Some of them were arduous undertakings.

Our expedition interested the Southampton people a good deal, and all wished us well; but I do not think many thought that we should be successful in realising our fortunes on Trinidad.

At last all was ready for our departure, when to my considerable disgust, just as we were about to put to sea, two of the volunteers suddenly found themselves prevented from going with us.

I forthwith telegraphed to others on my list of applicants, and at the very last moment received telegrams from two gentlemen who were willing to join at this short notice. When their messages arrived, all my crew and other companions were on board, comfortably settled down, having bidden their farewells and done with the shore; so I thought it prudent to send them away from Southampton, where the "Alerte" was perpetually surrounded by boatfuls of visitors, to the seclusion of the little bay under Calshot Castle at the mouth of Southampton Water. Here they would be out of the way of temptation, as there are no buildings save the coastguard station.

Therefore, on the evening of August 28, 1889, the "Alerte" sailed slowly down to Calshot, and came to an anchor there, while I waited at Southampton until the following morning, with the object of securing my new volunteers as soon as they should arrive, and carrying them down to the yacht.

The said volunteers turned up early on August 29. Then, with a party of some of my old Southampton friends, we steamed down the river on a launch which had been very kindly placed at our disposal for the purpose by the Isle of Wight Steamboat Company. Mr. Picket, of course, would have nothing to do with work in his yard on that day; he took a holiday and came down to see the last of us.

We were now all on board; but, finding that some of the fresh stores, such as vegetables and bread, had not yet arrived, we postponed our departure until the following day. In the meanwhile we were not idle; we sent a boat to the Hamble River to fill up those breakers which had been already emptied, we got our whale-boat on deck and secured it, and in short, made all ready for sea.

On the following day the Isle of Wight boat, while passing, left the missing stores with us; then Mr. Picket's sloop sailed down with some friends who had determined to bid us even yet another last farewell; and, after dinner, we weighed anchor and were off, while the friends on the sloop and the crew of a yacht which was brought up near us gave us a hearty good-bye in British cheers.

But our anchor had not yet had its last hold of English mud, and we were not to lose sight of the Solent that day; for, in consequence of some clumsiness, or possibly too much zeal on the part of those who were catting the anchor, the bowsprit whisker on the starboard side was doubled up; so we had to proceed to Cowes, and bring up there while we sent the iron on shore to be put in the fire and straightened again. However, this did not delay us much, for it fell a flat calm, which lasted through the night; we were better off sleeping comfortably at anchor than we should have been drifting helplessly up and down with the tides.

At 11 A.M. the next morning, it being high water, we weighed anchor, and were really off at last, the weather glorious and hot, but the wind light and variable.

For weeks, while we had been lying off Southampton, the weather had been detestable—blusterous north-west winds, accompanied by heavy rains, prevailing. But now, very opportunely for us, a complete change set in just as we started, and it was evident that we were at the commencement of a long spell of settled fine weather. I had anticipated this luck; for I knew by experience that the last weeks of August and the first weeks in September are the most favourable for a voyage south across the Bay, for then there generally comes a period of moderate easterly winds and warm weather, which precedes the stormy season of the equinox. Thus, when I sailed in the "Falcon" at this very time of the year, I was fortunate enough to carry a north-east wind all the way from Southampton into the north-east trades, and I was confident that we were destined to do something of the sort now; nor was I disappointed.

We got outside the Needles, and, the wind being light from west to south-west, we tacked very slowly down Channel, always in sight of the English coast, until nightfall, when the wind dropped altogether, and we lay becalmed in sight of Portland lights. It was our first Saturday night at sea (August 31), so we kept up the good old fashion of drinking to our wives and sweethearts at eight o'clock. We never neglected this sacred duty on any Saturday night during the whole cruise. A light air from the east sprang up at night, but, though we now had racing spinnaker and topsail on the vessel, we made little progress, and it seemed as if we could not lose sight of the lights of Portland.

Throughout the following day—September 1—the same far too fine weather continued, with light airs from various directions, alternating with calms. But we did at last contrive to get out of sight of land this day; Portland, to our delight, became invisible, and we saw no more of the English coast.

This calm weather was trying to the patience; but it was perhaps well for us to have this experience at the commencement of the voyage; for it enabled the raw hands to settle down to their work quickly, and there was but little sea-sickness on board.

At midday, September 2, we were off the chops of the Channel, a fresh easterly wind that lasted some hours having carried us so far. Then the wind fell again, and we sailed on in a very leisurely fashion until the morning of September 5, when, being well in the middle of the Bay of Biscay, the wind, which was from the south-east, began gradually to freshen. First we were going five knots through the water, then seven, and by midday we were travelling between eight and nine. In the afternoon the wind increased to the force of a moderate gale and the sea began to rise. During the night some rather high seas rolled up after us occasionally, so that we had to bear away and run before them, and only the old hands could be entrusted with the tiller. We passed Finisterre on this night, but were too far off to see the lights; and now we had done with the Bay of Biscay, which had certainly treated the "Alerte" with great consideration, and not shown us any of its proverbial bad temper. The wind had gone down by midday on the 6th, and the run for the previous twenty-four hours was found to have been 158 miles.

From this date we kept up a fair average speed; though our voyage could not be termed a smart one, for there was scarcely a day on which we were not retarded by several hours of calm.

While going down Channel we had kept watch and watch in the usual sea fashion, the first mate taking one watch and myself the other. But now that we were out at sea, clear of all danger, it became unnecessary to continue this somewhat wearisome four hours up and four hours down system; so we divided ourselves into three watches, the second mate taking the third watch. This gave the men an eight hours' rest below at a stretch, instead of only four. As we had three paid hands in addition to the cook, one of these was allotted to each watch. But before reaching the South American coast the second mate resigned his post, and we reverted to the watch-and-watch system again, which was observed until the termination of the cruise.

A good deal of useless form was kept up at this early stage of the voyage. A log-slate was suspended in the saloon, and each officer as he came below would write up a full account of all that had occurred in his watch. The most uninteresting details were minutely chronicled—only to be rubbed off the

slate each midday, and I think there was a little disappointment expressed because I would not copy all these down in my
log-book. Had I done so that log-book would have been a
dreadful volume to peruse.

To us, however, the log-slate was a source of great amusement on account of its utter fallaciousness. The patent log
was, of course, put overboard when we were making the land,
but when we were out on the ocean and no land was near us
we naturally did not take the trouble to do this, neither did
we make use of the common log-ship or keep a strict dead
reckoning. But, despite this, the officer of a watch would
religiously jot down the exact number of knots and furlongs
he professed to have sailed during each of his four hours on
duty; he did not even try to guess the distance to the best of
his ability; he was fired with an ambition to show the best
record for his watch; so he would first scan the slate to see how
many knots the officer just relieved boasted to have accomplished, and then he would unblushingly write down a slightly
greater number of miles as the result of his own watch, quite
regardless of any fall in the wind or other retarding cause.

Thus: if five knots an hour had been made in one watch,
five and a quarter would probably be logged for the next, and
five and a half for the next. Sometimes there was a flat calm
throughout a watch, and then the ingenious officer, though he
could not help himself and was compelled to write himself
down a zero before three of the hours, would compensate for
this by putting down a big number in front of that hour during
which he imagined that all the individuals of his rival watches
were fast asleep below, and would boldly assert in explanation
that just then he had been favoured with a strong squall to
help him along.

No one put any confidence in this mendacious slate, which
soon became known on board as the "Competition Log," and
inspired our wits with many merry quips. The distance made
in each twenty-four hours as recorded by the Competition
Log was about fifty per cent. greater than that calculated
from observations of the sun.

At last, on the morning of September 13, having been

fourteen days at sea, and having accomplished a voyage of something under fifteen hundred miles, we knew that we were in the close vicinity of the Salvages, and a sharp look-out for land was accordingly kept. We had seen nothing but water round us since leaving Portland Bill, and all on board were excited at the prospect of so soon discovering what manner of place was this desert treasure-island of which we had been talking so much.

The Salvages lie between Madeira and the Canaries, being 160 miles from the former and about 85 from Teneriffe. Vessels avoid their vicinity, especially at night, on account of the dangerous shoals that surround them. The description of the group in the "North Atlantic Memoir" is as follows:—

"The Salvages consist of an island named the Ilha Grande, or the Great Salvage, a larger island named Great Piton, and a smaller one called the Little Piton, together with several rocks. The Great Salvage lies in lat. 30° 8', long, 15° 55'. It is of very irregular shape, and has a number of rocks about it within the distance of a mile. It is much intersected, and has several deep inlets, the most accessible of which is on the east side. It is covered with bushes, amongst which the thousands of sea-fowl make their nests. It is surrounded on all sides with dangers, most of which show, but many require all caution in approaching.

"The Great Piton lies at the distance of $8\frac{1}{4}$ miles W.S.W. $\frac{3}{4}$ W. from Ilha Grande. This islet is $2\frac{3}{8}$ miles long, and has a hill or peak near its centre. The Little Piton lies at a mile from the western side of the former, and is three-quarters of a mile long; both are comparatively narrow. These isles are seated upon and surrounded by one dangerous rocky bank, which extends from the western side of the little isle half a league to the westward." . . . "The southern part of the Great Piton appears green, its northern part barren. It may be seen 5 or 6 leagues off. The Little Piton is very flat, and is connected to the south point of the greater one by a continued ledge of rocks. The whole of the eastern side of the Great Piton is rocky and dangerous."

A light north-east trade-wind was blowing, and we were

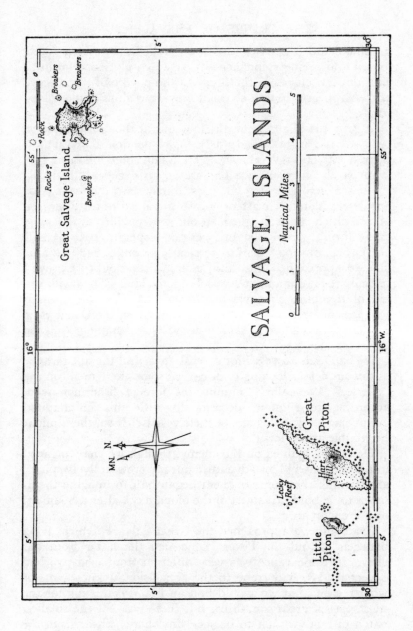

SALVAGE ISLANDS

Nautical Miles

0　1　2　3　4　5

Great Salvage Island

Rocks?

Rock

Breakers

Breakers

Breakers

16°

16° W.

MN. N.

Lecky Reef

Great Piton

Hart Hills

Little Piton

running before it at a fair rate through the smooth water, with topsail and racing spinnaker set. It w. a glorious morning, with but few clouds in the sky, and those were of that fleecy, broken appearance that characterises the regions of the trade-winds.

At 8.30 A.M. the man on the look out at the crosstrees sang out:—"Land right ahead, sir!" Yes—no doubt about it—there it was, still several leagues off, a faint blue hill of rugged form on the horizon; we had made an excellent land-fall. While we were straining our eyes to make out the features of our desert island, our attention was attracted to a still nearer object which suddenly gleamed out snowy white as the sun's rays fell on it, triangular in form and appearing like a small chalk rock, but too far off to be clearly distinguished. Gradually we approached this, and, after a little doubt, it proved to be no rock, but a sailing-vessel of some kind. Then with the aid of the binoculars we made her out; she was a small schooner of foreign rig, evidently hailing from the Canaries or Madeiras, and she was sailing as we were, shaping a course direct for the island.

We had seen no vessel for several days, and the appearance of this suspicious-looking craft caused some excitement on the "Alerte." We called to mind the foreign fishermen who, according to rumour, occasionally visit this uninhabited archipelago. Was this one of their vessels? If so, there might be trouble ahead for us.

We rapidly gained on the enemy, though we were engaged in a stern chase. This adventure put my crew in lively spirits, and I think that some of them began half to imagine themselves to be bold privateers of the olden days, after a Spaniard or a Frenchman.

Gradually we approached the Great Salvage, which, lying between us and the Pitons, concealed the latter from our view. Its appearance was very different from what we had expected. We had come to the conclusion, I know not for what reason, that we should find an island consisting for the most part of great sand-hills; but there was not the smallest patch of sandy beach to be seen anywhere. Sheer from the

46

sea rose great rocks of volcanic formation, dark and rugged; and, though we were still several miles off, we could perceive that the sea was breaking heavily on every part of the weather coast, for we could hear the booming of the rollers and see the frequent white flash of the foam against the black cliff-sides. But above these precipices towards the centre of the island there was a plateau, or rather an undulating green down, with one steep green dome dominating all, looking very fresh and pleasant to eyes that for two weeks had only gazed at the monotonous plains of the sea.

As I have already explained, my informant from Exeter was of opinion that the "Prometheus" people were wrong in digging on the shores of the Great Salvage, and that the treasure had been concealed on the Great Piton or middle island. We decided in the first place to come to an anchor off the Great Salvage, and after having explored that island, to sail for the Great Piton.

According to the Admiralty charts there are two anchorages off the Great Salvage, one in the East Bay and one in the South Bay. We accordingly steered so as to coast down the east side of the island, and thus open out both of these inlets.

At midday we were not quite a league astern of the schooner. She was close under the north point of the island, when suddenly she hauled her wind and steered in a westerly direction, seemingly for the open sea; so we came to the conclusion that our excitement had been groundless, and that in all probability we should not be troubled by inquisitive foreigners during our exploration of the Salvages.

We soon found that it was necessary to exercise considerable caution while approaching this island. Nearly two miles away from it there was a shoal over which the sea was breaking heavily; we passed between this and the island as directed by the chart, and kept close under the shore, where the dark violet of the deep sea was changed for the transparent green of comparatively shallow water. Here again we had to pick our way through outlying rocks and shoals. One of these shoals is particularly dangerous, for, as there is some depth of water over it, the sea only occasionally breaks, and for a quarter of an hour at a time there is nothing to indicate the danger, so that a vessel might through inadvertence, be taken right on to it.

When we were close to it the sea happened to break, and the sight was a lovely, yet a terrible one. A huge green roller, very high and steep, suddenly rose as if by magic from the deep; then swept over the shoal, and, when it reached the shallowest part, its crest hung over, forming a cavern underneath, through whose transparent roof the sun shone with a beautiful green light; and lastly, the mass overtopping itself fell with a great hollow sound, and was dashed to pieces in a whirl of hissing foam. Had the old "Alerte" been there at that moment her end would have come swiftly, and perhaps ours too.

The chart seems to mark these rocks and breakers very correctly, and there is small danger of falling a victim to them if proper precautions are observed. Besides which, the water is so clear that one can see through it many fathoms down, and a man in the cross-trees with an eye experienced to the work could always detect a danger in good time.

We rounded the north-east point and opened East Bay. We did not like the look of the anchorage here, which is in ten fathoms, and could see no good landing nor any signs of a sandy beach; so we sailed on and doubled the south-east point and the shoals that extend some way from it, suddenly opening out South Bay, the one in which it seems that the "Prometheus" came to an anchor.

And then, to our astonishment, we beheld a very unexpected sight. Rolling easily on the green ocean swell, at some three cables' length from the shore, lay a small schooner at anchor; her crew—a half naked, bronzed, and savage-looking lot— were engaged in stowing her mainsail. She was evidently the same schooner we had seen outside. While we had been coasting round the east side of the island she had followed the west side, and here we had met again. But she was not the only surprise in store for us. There were no sandy dunes in this bay; its shores were steep and rocky, and on either side reefs, on which the sea broke, protected the anchorage to some extent. At the head of one picturesque cove, wherein was evidently the best landing-place, were two small huts, put together of rough stones from the beach, and from these a footpath wound up the bare volcanic cliffs to the green plateau some four hundred feet above. A quantity of barrels were being quickly landed here from one of the schooner's boats, and several other wild-looking men were carrying these up to a cavern a little way up the rocks behind the huts. The whole formed a wild and fantastic picture. It was just such a scene as Salvator Rosa would have delighted to paint, it would have suited the savage austerity of his style. The rugged cove might well have been the haunt of smugglers or pirates. And who, we wondered, were these people, and what were they doing; these were mysterious proceedings for a desert island! The evident labour of the men while carrying the barrels proved to us that they were very heavy. "Perhaps," suggested one of us—"perhaps we have just arrived at the right moment to interrupt another band of pirates in the act of hiding another immense treasure."

This would have been almost too great a stroke of luck for my band of adventurers. It would have been very pleasant to have saved ourselves all the trouble of digging, and to have simply carried off the evilly earned hoard of these wicked men and divided it among our virtuous selves. We had sanguine men on board whom no failure disheartened, despite their invariable habit of counting their chickens before they were hatched; so I was not surprised to be now asked by the sportsman of our party how long I thought it would take us to get back to England. When I had replied, he evinced great satisfaction. "Oh, that is all right then!" he said. "We can get this stuff on board and be back home just in time for the pheasant-shooting; and, after that, we can fit out again and fetch our other treasures."

We came to an anchor in seven fathoms of water a short distance outside the schooner. It was not the sort of roadstead I should like to remain long in; for an iron-bound shore was before us, and around were numerous shoals on which the rollers kept up a perpetual hullaballoo—a nasty trap to be caught in should the wind suddenly veer to the southward.

It was after one o'clock when we brought up, so we decided to go below and dine before doing anything else, and the conversation at table became more piratical in its tone than ever. After the details of how we were to enrich ourselves despite all obstacles had been thoroughly discussed, each of the adventurers explained in what way he would spend his share of the booty: how it should be invested was, of course, far too prosaic a matter for his consideration.

CHAPTER VI

ON THE SALVAGES

As soon as dinner was over the whale-boat was put into the water, and I pulled off to the landing-place with two of my companions.

The men on shore were still employed in carrying the barrels up to the cavern, but when we approached they ceased working, and stood gazing at us, with a not unnatural curiosity. We found the landing-place to be a queer one. A little channel clove the rocks for sixty or seventy feet inland. This inlet was so narrow that there was scarce room within it to work a boat with oars, and, as the ocean swell entered it with sufficient force to render a collision with the rocks dangerous for any boat, an ingenious arrangement had been placed there to facilitate the landing. Just outside the entrance of the inlet a barrel floated, which was moored to a big stone or anchor at the bottom; a stout grass rope was attached to this barrel, and the other end of it was made fast to a rock on shore at the head of the inlet. By hauling along this rope, which was sufficiently taut for the purpose, the boat was kept well in the centre of the channel and all risk of getting foul of the rocks on either side was avoided. At the end of the inlet was a rocky shelf, on to which we jumped, having first made our boat fast to the rope in such a way that she could not bump against the shore.

Then there came down to us a very brown and amiable-looking old gentleman, whose dress consisted solely of a short, ragged shirt, which had once, I think, been of a vivid green, but which had now been toned down to a more æsthetic tint with age and dirt. He welcomed us to the island by silently shaking each of us by the hand very cordially.

I addressed him in Spanish, but he shook his head and commenced to speak in a language which I recognised as a Portuguese patois of some description. But we soon contrived to understand each other fairly well. He told me that he was the padron of the wild crew, who stood round listening to our conversation with grave faces—a sort of governor of the islet, and chief owner of the barrels of wealth which lay before us. He was also captain of the schooner.

Then he beckoned to us to follow him, and he led us into one of the stone huts, the furniture of which consisted of barrels like those that were being landed from the schooner, an open hogshead of black grapes and a demijohn. The good old man pulled out a pannikin from between the stones of the wall, and proceeded to serve out to each of us a tot of excellent aguardiente from the demijohn.

One of the half-naked men happened to be bringing another of the mysterious barrels into the hut; so, without showing any impolite curiosity, I contrived to hint that I should like to know what it contained. The padron forthwith dipped the pannikin into a barrel that had been already broached, and poured the contents into my hand. It was, as I had expected, not pirate treasure, but coarse salt.

Then he explained to me that he and his companions were natives of Madeira, that they were in the habit of coming here with their schooner at this season of the year, and that they made this bay their headquarters for salting down the fish which they caught, but that for the remainder of the year there were no human beings on these islands. He further said that the Salvages were claimed by the Portuguese, and not by the Spanish. On being asked whether there was any fresh water on the island, he said there was a small fountain in a hollow on the summit, and that all the water they used had to be brought down from there in small breakers on the heads of his men. They were nimble enough in scrambling down the cliffs under their burdens, as we saw later on; but all Madeirans are excellent mountaineers.

Then the padron, looking rather sly, enquired in his turn:— "What have you Englishmen come here for? It is rare that vessels come by here."

"It is on our way to Teneriffe," I replied, "and as this is a pleasure yacht we are not bound to time."

"Once before an Englishman came here. I thought you might have come for the same reason as he."

"And why did he come?"

"To look for hidden money."

This was very interesting, but we tried to assume a look of innocent surprise, as if we had heard nothing of this before.

"There is a great treasure hidden on this island somewhere," he continued, "and the English know of it. Some years ago this milord came with his yacht, a bigger one than yours, a steamer with three masts, and they dug for the treasure. Oh! it is a great treasure, more than a thousand English pounds they say; but the Englishmen did not find it."

"Where did they dig?" I asked.

"I do not know. I was not on the island at the time. It was several years ago."

That was all he seemed to know; we could elicit no further information on the subject from him; but it was evident that the "Alerte" was not the first yacht that had come to the Salvages in search of the hidden chests of dollars.

We then set forth to explore the island. We climbed the narrow path that zigzagged up the bare cliffs, and in the construction of which a considerable amount of labour must have been expended, a proof in itself that the rare visitors to the island were Portuguese, for these people alone take the trouble to make roads on desert islands. They seem to love for its own sake the arduous work of cutting paths up difficult precipices, and very cleverly they do it too. We came across the remains of excellent Portuguese roads even among the apparently inaccessible crags of Trinidad.

We reached the green downs on the summit. The sky was cloudless and a fresh breeze was blowing over the sea, so the tramp was very enjoyable to us after the cramped life on board a small vessel.

On every portion of these downs we found walls roughly put together of piled up stones, which in some places formed long parallel lines, in others square enclosures. The object of these had probably been to prevent the soil from being washed into the sea; but whatever cultivation had formerly been carried on here had evidently been abandoned long since, in consequence, no doubt, of the insufficiency of the water-supply. The fishermen appeared to be entirely ignorant of the history of these old walls. In one place there were traces of an ancient vineyard. Wherever the ground was not too stony a coarse grass grew luxuriantly over the downs. There were also wild tomatoes in profusion and alkaline sea plants of various species.

We saw many rabbits dodging among the rocks, and gulls and cormorants in quantities. The cormorants dwelt with their families in fine stone houses which they had constructed with great ingenuity. Some of the stones were large and heavy; it would be interesting to observe how the birds set to work to move these and how they put their roofs on. I have been told that they rake up a mound of stones with their powerful wings in such a way that by removing some of those underneath they leave the roof above them. The gulls are not such good architects as the cormorants, and for the most part live in the natural crevices of the rocks, or in holes which they steal from the rabbits. We, however, saw one conscientious gull in the act of making his own house. He had selected a large stone lying on soft soil, and was burrowing a deep cavern underneath it.

We walked round the downs, looking over the cliffs into every bay; but we could see no extensive sandy beach such as that described by Captain Robinson. There were small patches of sand here and there, and that was all. The shore was formed of rock and shingle. It is probable that many changes have taken place on this exposed islet since the visit of the "Prometheus"; the sands may have been washed away, and there is no doubt that rocks and rocky landslips are constantly falling from above.

We saw clearly that it would be useless for us to dig in any of these bays; for none of them corresponded with the description given by the Spanish sailor; so we came to the conclusion that our search must be undertaken, if anywhere, on the middle island and not on the Great Salvage.

When on the summit of the island we looked out towards

the south for the famous Peak of Teneriffe, which is said to be sometimes visible at a distance of one hundred and fifty miles. We were not much more than eighty miles from it here and the day was quite clear, but we could see no signs of it; neither was it visible while we were on the Great Piton, which is eight miles nearer. I have been at sea in the neighbourhood of Teneriffe on several occasions, but have never yet had a view of the great mountain, so either I am very unlucky or it must be rare indeed that it is to be distinguished at anything like the distance alleged.

Having explored the islet, we proceeded to hunt rabbits. We had brought no guns with us, so tried to kill them with stones, but failed completely; we were all out of practice at this sort of sport. We then descended the path to the huts, where the padron gave us a smiling welcome, and, inviting us again into the hut, produced for our benefit an unwonted luxury, a bottle of rough Madeira. We purchased some grapes from him and a bottle of aguardiente, and, having bade farewell to our Portuguese friends, we pulled off to the yacht and recounted our adventures to the others.

When we tasted the aguardiente we discovered that the monarch of the desert island understood how to trade in quite a civilised fashion; it was horrible stuff, not at all up to the excellent sample he had treated us to on our landing.

Shortly before sunset the schooner, having discharged all her salt, weighed anchor and set sail for Madeira, leaving about six men behind on the island.

As some of my companions seemed rather keen on taking their guns on shore and having a few hours' rabbit-shooting, I decided that the yacht should remain at anchor where she was during the following forenoon, so as to enable them to enjoy their sport and stock our larder with fresh meat—a very acceptable luxury—while I would sail with a few hands in the whale-boat at daybreak to the Great Piton, effect a landing there if possible, and discover whether there was any bay which answered to the Spanish sailor's description. In the afternoon the yacht was to get under weigh, and rejoin me at the other island.

So at 4 o'clock the next morning, September 14, we had coffee, put some provisions and two breakers of water into the boat, together with a few picks and shovels, a compass and other necessaries, and then sailed away.

I left the first mate in charge of the yacht, having first arranged a short code of signals with him, so that I could communicate from the shore when the yacht appeared off the Great Piton.

I took one of the signal code flags with me, which when flying from a perpendicular staff was to signify "All Right," two waves of the flag indicated that we were coming off to the yacht in the boat, four waves was an order to the mate to send the dinghy off to us, and eight or more waves meant that we had found a likely-looking place and that I had decided to carry on digging operations. We were to indicate the best anchorage by pointing the flag in the direction we wished the yacht to be steered.

It was still dark when we got under weigh in the whale-boat, so the binnacle light was lit, and we shaped our course by compass towards the still invisible island, which was about nine miles distant.

I had with me the doctor, the second mate, and one of the paid hands—Arthur Cotton. When we got clear of the protecting island we found that a fresh wind was blowing nearly right aft; so we set the two sprit sails and ran fast across a tumbling sea, the Atlantic swell looking formidable when our little boat was in the deep hollows between the lofty crests.

By-and-by a faint light appeared in the east, and a red, rather stormy-looking dawn broadened across the dark sky.

Shortly after sunrise, the mists clearing from the islet, we perceived the Great Piton right ahead of us; but we only caught sight of it when we were on the summits of the waves, losing it again when we were in the deep valleys between.

We scudded on, and as we approached nearer, the sea became more confused and a little water tumbled on board occasionally. Outlying rocks showed their black heads above the water here and there, while curling breakers indicated the presence of other invisible dangers.

We lowered our sails and inspected the island from a safe distance before venturing to land; for if proper precautions are not exercised it is a very easy matter to lose one's boat in a moment while beaching on any of these small oceanic islets.

We saw that the Great Piton was much lower than the Great Salvage, the shore was rocky and indented, and there was a good deal of surf in places. Above the shore was a green undulating plain, while towards the middle of it rose a steep dome with dark rocks at the summit.

The average height of the plain above the sea seemed to be about twenty feet, and the central hill, according to the chart, is only 140 feet high. We observed that there were sandy beaches in many of the little coves, and some of these tallied well with the spot described by the Spaniard.

The Great Piton, as will be seen by reference to the chart, is a long narrow island extending from north-east to south-west magnetic; therefore the whole side facing the south-east could be accurately described as the south side. It was somewhere on this shore that the mutineers must have landed with the chests.

Picking our way through the outer shoals we made for what appeared to be the best landing-place, a snug little cove at the eastern extremity of this south side. Here we landed without any difficulty; but, finding it impossible to haul our heavy boat up the beach, we moored her safely in the bay and waded on shore with our stores.

On a sandy slope above the rocks we found the ruined walls of a stone hut. By placing our sails over these we made a snug little house. "And now," cried our medical adviser, "I suggest that, before doing anything else, we have breakfast." Our early morning sail on the ocean had given us all a hearty appetite, so a fire was lit, cocoa made, and the ship biscuits and tinned beef were duly appreciated. Then we enjoyed our pipes, and leaving Arthur behind to make the camp as comfortable as he could, we set forth to explore the island. Our first discovery was that the corner on which we had landed became a separate islet at high water; for it was divided from the bulk of the Great Piton by a broad depression, across which at about three-quarters flood the sea rushed with a violent current. This depression was of rock and lava, and it had been worn into a smooth and level floor by the action of innumerable tides. At low water it was several feet above the sea, so that one could then walk across dry shod.

We walked along the whole southern shore of the island, and it appeared to us that there were at least three coves to which the Spaniard's description could apply equally well. We found no inhabitants, but there were frequent signs of the Portuguese fishermen who occasionally visit the islet. We saw many footprints on the sand, showing that some men had been here very recently. We came across their rough stone huts full of fleas, some of their fishing-tackle, mounds of coarse salt, the ashes of their fires, and in one cavern there were stored the large iron pots in which they cooked their food.

We found no rabbits on the island, and very few birds. The sole creatures on shore were beetles, flies, and fleas. The latter lively insects were a great plague to us at night, it was unwise of us to pitch our camp in the hut of a Portuguese fisherman. On the beach were great numbers of very active little crabs. There was no fresh water on the island.

We ascended the peak, which is named Hart Hill on the chart. Its top is formed of rugged masses of coal-black rock, evidently of volcanic formation, and this is studded with large black crystals, like plums in a plum-pudding. These crystals attracted our attention at once. We chipped off some and found them hard and heavy. We began to speculate on the nature of this substance, and as none of us knew much of mineralogy we of course at once decided, in our usual sanguine way, that this must be an oxide of antimony, or manganese, or some other valuable product. There were thousands of tons of this stuff on the island, so we clearly saw our way to another vast fortune of a different description to that we were seeking. It was settled that we would obtain a concession from the Portuguese before the value of our find leaked out, then we would sell our rights to an English company or syndicate for an immense sum. We sat there on the top of our crystalline treasure and arranged it all. "It might be worth while," suggested one humdrum individual, "in the first place to send a specimen home to be assayed, so that we may form some approximate idea of the extent of our fortunes; but we must send it to some person whom we can rely upon not to breathe a word of the secret and so stop our chances of making an advantageous bargain with the Portuguese."

Later on, when we reached Teneriffe, we did send some of the crystals home, and when we arrived at Bahia we were informed by letter of the result of the assay and of the exact market value per ton of the stuff.

But I will not keep any of my friends who may read this book in suspense. They need not apply to me for an early allotment of shares in the great syndicate. We have not made our fortunes just yet. I will anticipate by giving the assayist's report. It ran thus:—"Volcanic hornblende. Commercial value—nil."

But we did not waste much time in building our castles in the air, and returned to business.

Looking from the summit of our hornblende peak the whole island lay stretched out before us like a map, and we could easily distinguish all the features of the Little Piton, which seemed to be about two miles away. On the Admiralty chart the coast and shoals of the Great Salvage are correctly drawn; but this cannot be said of the plan of the Great Piton: this is utterly unreliable. The survey does not profess to be more than a superficial one, but great changes must have occurred here since it was made. There are not wanting signs that the sea has encroached a great deal on the land, and that it is still doing so. In the first place the island is not three miles long, as shown on the chart, its length cannot exceed one mile and a half. The shores, again, are far more irregular in shape, the outer islands and shoals more numerous, than the chart indicates. Perhaps these last have been cut off the island by the sea since the survey. We perceived that the sea was breaking all round the island on far projecting promontories and shallow reefs; but, strangely enough, where the chart does mark one well-defined continuous reef joining the Great

Piton to the Little Piton, there appeared to be a broad open channel of deep water.

We saw one likely-looking bay to the southward of our camp, so, while we were waiting for the yacht, the three of us set to with our shovels, and dug parallel trenches in the sand at right angles to the shore, working upwards from a short distance above high water mark. We did not dig these trenches to a greater depth than three feet, for we then came to a hard soil which to all appearance had never been disturbed. We found it pretty hard work under that fiery subtropical sun, unaccustomed as we were to the use of pick and shovel.

In the afternoon the yacht appeared off the island; so we signalled to her with the flag in the preconcerted manner: "Come to an anchor." "We will pass the night on shore;" and, whereas eight or more waves of the flag were to signify that we had found a likely place for the hidden treasure, we waved most energetically for quite two minutes—a sanguine signal that must have led my companions on board to conclude that we had at least discovered the first of the chests of dollars.

The yacht came to an anchor off the bay at which we had first landed. The mate came off to us in the dinghy, and I told him our plans and instructed him to send other hands off to us in the morning, together with all necessary stores. He then returned to the yacht, while we passed the night in our hut in the company of the innumerable sleepless fleas.

Early on the following morning—September 15—the boat came off with five more of my companions, which raised our shore party to nine.

We then shifted our camp from the torture hut of fleas to a sandy spot further to the southward under Hart Hill, and here we pitched the two emigrant tents which had been brought for Trinidad. The boat returned to the yacht for the stores, and brought back to us all the picks, shovels, and crowbars, a forty-gallon tank of water, and plenty of provisions, including a savoury stew of Salvagee rabbits, for our sportsmen had had good luck on the previous day.

After the camp had been put in order the whole party set

forth to survey the southern shore, and each, having read the Spaniard's narrative, gave his opinion as to the most likely spot.

Then we arranged a methodical plan of action, and his portion of work was allotted to each man. We dug trenches in parallel lines in some places, in others we drew them in A shapes, gold prospector's fashion, generally working in a sandy earth, but sometimes through shingle.

The surface of the island has, no doubt, undergone many changes since 1804, the year in which it is alleged that the treasure was buried. It was therefore often difficult to decide to what depth the trenches should be dug; for we came to a hard, darker soil, which some of us considered to be of ancient formation, undisturbed for centuries, while others were of opinion that loose sand mixing with vegetable matter could easily have consolidated into this in the course of eighty years. When we had dug the trenches as far down as we intended we sounded the earth to a still greater depth by driving in the crowbars at short intervals. At one time some excitement was caused by the discovery of bones, but our doctor pronounced them to be the bones of a whale and not of a human being.

By dinner time we had dug a goodly array of trenches; for we were working energetically despite the burning sun.

While we were enjoying an interval of rest after the midday meal and smoking our pipes, I took those of the working party who had not yet seen the black crystals, to the summit of Hart Hill, and asked their opinion of the mineral. None of them had seen a rock of like formation before, and they thought this might prove a valuable discovery. Our sportsman took in the value of the hill at a glance. "Well," he said, "I don't think so much of this as of the other treasures. However, it may be worth a quarter of a million or so to us. I will put my share of it on 'X' for the Derby." I may mention that the horse he selected did not turn out to be this year's Derby winner.

We worked steadily through the afternoon, also for the whole of the next day, September 16. On this day the mate reported that the remainder of our salt beef, some 400 pounds, was spoiled. It had, accordingly, to be thrown overboard.

It was just possible that the treasure had been hidden on the Little Piton, and not on the island on which we were working. The Little Piton might be described as the middle island, for it lies between the Great Piton and another small islet or rock, apparently not marked in the chart; while the Great Salvage is as often as not invisible from here.

So on the morning of September 17, leaving the other hands to continue the trenches, I sailed in the whale-boat with two of my companions to the Little Piton. We found that this islet also had a sandy down in its centre; but after several trials we saw that it was impossible to effect a landing on any part of it. There was no snug little cove, such as the one described by Cruise. The sea was breaking in an ugly way along the rocky coast, and the water round the islet was so thickly studded with rocks and reefs that it was dangerous to approach it.

After inspecting the shore as closely as we dared we abandoned the attempt and, setting sail, hurried back to the Great Piton; for the sky looked stormy to windward, and a heavy rain-squall came up which for a time hid all land from our sight—not desirable weather for cruising about the Atlantic in an open boat, for should a strong wind rise we should be unable to make any way against it, and might easily be blown away from the islets out to sea.

We landed again safely on the Great Piton, and after digging for some more hours, we sat together in council, and upon a little discussion it was unanimously decided that it was not worth our while to carry on any further operations on the Salvages. We had already dug hard for four days and might easily dig for forty more without having explored more than a small fraction of the sandy beaches on the south side of the island. Besides this there existed a considerable doubt whether this was the right island at all. The information was of far too vague a nature, our chance of success far too remote to encourage us to stay longer. Moreover, the anchorage was a very unsafe one should it come on to blow, and even now the glass was falling rapidly and the sky looked ominous.

I had originally intended to sail for St. Vincent in the Cape

Verde islands, and had indeed directed letters to be forwarded to us there; but this island was still a thousand miles distant, and, seeing that we had lost all our salt beef and had consumed a good deal of our water—the digging on the island under the sun had, of course, produced great thirst—it became almost necessary to call for provisions at some nearer port than St. Vincent.

I accordingly decided to sail for Santa Cruz on Teneriffe, which is less than a day's sail from the Great Piton, if one have any luck in one's winds.

So we broke up our camp, struck the tents, carried everybody and everything on board in two journeys of the boat, then got both boats on board and made all ready for sea.

With the exception of the Salvages, I had before visited every place at which we called with the "Alerte"; and even the Salvages were not entirely new to me, for I had seen them from the deck of the steam-yacht "Sans Peur" in 1885, when she was on her way from Madeira to Teneriffe.

This cruise consequently was not quite so fresh and interesting to me as to my companions, and would have seemed almost a dull one had it not been for the excitement of treasure-hunting.

CHAPTER VII

RUNNING DOWN THE TRADES

At four in the afternoon we hoisted the sails and weighed the anchor. I was at the helm at the time and was very surprised at the extraordinary manner in which the vessel now behaved. She seemed bewitched; a nice breeze was blowing, her sails were full, and yet she gathered no way on her, forged not a foot ahead, but remained where she was, tumbling about uneasily on the long ground-swell.

She was acting for all the world like an obstinate buck-jumping horse. Never before had the amiable old yawl evinced any signs of temper, and this display grieved me much, for I had thought better of her.

This strange behaviour went on for quite a minute, when suddenly she seemed to come to her senses, gave herself a shake, and with a quick leap darted ahead and was rushing through the water in her usual steady style.

One of the crew now happened to look over the side, and called the attention of the others to something that he saw dangling there. There was a roar of laughter. The good old vessel had been cruelly wronged by our suspicions; she was entirely innocent of obstinacy or temper of any sort. Our purser alone was to blame for what had occurred. He was a most energetic but unsuccessful fisherman, and had come on board at Southampton well provided with fishing tackle of all descriptions; he was prepared for every inhabitant of the deep, from the narwhal and the whale to whelks and whitebait. So on this afternoon, while we were getting ready for sea, he had been vainly attempting to catch sharks with a bit of our condemned beef as bait, and had forgotten to take his line on board when we got under weigh. The stout shark hook had got hold of the rocks at the bottom and had securely anchored us by the stern. The strong line held well, but something had to give way before the increasing straining of the vessel as the wind filled her sails; on hauling in the line we found that one arm of the hook had broken off and so released us.

At sunset the desert islets faded out of sight, and we sailed on through the night across a smooth sea with a light westerly breeze on our beam.

That we failed to discover the treasure on the Salvages did not dishearten my companions in the least. It is true that all had realized beforehand how remote were our chances of success; still, it was very encouraging to find that there was no grumbling or expression of disappointment after those four days of hard digging in vain under a hot sun: it argued well for the way in which these men would face the far greater difficulties of Trinidad.

On the following morning, September 18, we caught sight of the Peak of Teneriffe, about twenty miles distant. We sailed past the north point of the island, coasted by the volcanic mountains that, with their barren inhospitable crags, give so little indication of the fertile vales within, and came to an anchor at 2 P.M. off Santa Cruz.

The Port doctor immediately came off to us, and was quite satisfied with my bill of health for Sydney, and my explanation that we had called here for provisions and water; so he gave us pratique without demur.

Then land-clothes were donned, and some of my companions went on shore to enjoy the luxuries of civilisation once again.

Santa Cruz is a pleasant little place, and seemed to me to have improved a good deal since my last visit. The hotels at any rate are far better than they were; I remember that it was once impossible to get a decent meal in the town, but we were now quite satisfied with the International Hotel in the Plaza. It is under English management, and several of our countrymen and countrywomen were passing the winter there. Some of my companions dined at this hotel on every night during our stay, and expressed themselves well contented with the table; like all pirates, they were, of course, great gourmets while on shore and knew the difference between good and bad.

We remained a week at Santa Cruz, being delayed by a

variety of causes, so some of the party were enabled to travel over the island on donkeys and see its peculiar scenery.

A very sharp little ragged boy took a great fancy to the "Alerte" crew. He insisted on protecting the innocent foreigners and acting as their cicerone when they walked about the town. He drove all other beggars and loafers away from them, and even bullied the sentries when they raised objections to a couple of my men trespassing on the forbidden precincts of the citadel. This urchin was afraid of no one and was very intelligent; as few of us understood his Spanish, he communicated all that he had to say by means of a most expressive pantomime. It was grand to observe his apologetic manner when he took us into the cathedral and showed us the flags that had been captured from Nelson during his disastrous attack on Teneriffe in 1797. He looked up into our faces with a solemn and sympathetic look. He would not hurt our feelings for worlds.

The ragged urchins of Santa Cruz are as like each other as so many John Chinamen; so, when our own particular boy was not by, some other would come to us with a welcoming smile and attempt to impersonate him. Therefore, in order to distinguish our own from his pretenders, we decorated him with an old brass button, which he wore proudly on his breast.

I will not attempt here a description of this so often described island. In my opinion it must be a far pleasanter winter resort than that somewhat melancholy island Madeira, where there is a depressing sense of being imprisoned by the steep mountains. The mountains of Teneriffe are still higher, but there are broad and beautiful plains beneath them that give an idea of freedom and breathing-room. There are excellent hotels in other portions of Teneriffe, and in the neighbourhood of Santa Cruz there are many beautifully situated villas and châteaux belonging to the native gentry that can be hired at very moderate rates indeed, while provisions are good and cheap.

The ship's complement was diminished by two at Santa Cruz, the boatswain and one of the volunteers leaving us.

Before sailing we took on board a large quantity of stores,

including barrels of salt beef which proved to be of a very inferior quality to that we had brought from Southampton, but this was ancient, and, having arrived at a certain stage of nastiness, was not likely to get any worse. The paid hands quite approved of it, for it was at any rate better than that served out on the majority of merchant vessels. We also procured some very fair native wine, like a rough port, which, mixed with water, formed a wholesome drink for the tropics. The high temperature we experienced while crossing the equator nearly spoiled this, so that we had to fortify it further with rum in order to preserve it. On the last day of our stay we went to the excellent fruit market, and laid in a good supply of grapes, bananas, and other fruits and vegetables. We also purchased a quantity of the cheap native cigars; so for a while we lived luxuriously on board ship.

I would have sailed from here direct for Bahia, at which port—as being the nearest to Trinidad—it was my intention to fill up with water and other necessaries before commencing our chief operations; but as letters were awaiting many of us at St. Vincent in the Cape Verdes I decided to call at that island on the way.

At 9 A.M., September 25, we weighed anchor and sailed to St. Vincent. The distance is a little under 900 miles, which we accomplished in seven days.

For the first three days we encountered south to south-east winds, with fine weather. On September 28 the wind veered to the north-east, being thus right aft. As the boom of our racing spinnaker was a very heavy spar and formed a considerable top weight while standing along the mainmast in the usual way, we unshipped it from its gooseneck and laid it on deck.

We had now come into a region of strong trades. The wind was fresh and squally and we ran through the night with the tack of our mainsail triced well up and our mizen stowed.

On the following day, September 29, the glass was still falling, and the sea running up astern of us was occasionally high and steep. There were signs of worse weather coming, so we prepared for it by striking the topmast, lowering our main-sail and setting our trysail. The day's run was 174 miles.

The glass had given us a false alarm after all; for on the following day the wind moderated, and we were enabled to hoist our large balloon foresail; but a heavy sea was still rolling up from the north-east. It was evident that a gale had been recently blowing over the disturbed tract of ocean which we were now crossing.

The Cape Verde islands are frequently enveloped in clouds, so that they cannot be distinguished until one is quite close to them. This had been my former experience and the same thing occurred now. In the night of October 1 we knew that we were in the vicinity of the island of St. Antonio, the northern-most of the archipelago, but right ahead of us there stretched a great bank of cloud, concealing everything behind. At last, however, a squall partly cleared the rolling vapour and we perceived, a few miles distant, the black mountainous mass of the island, whose volcanic peaks rise to a height of upwards of 7,000 feet above the sea. Then the bright flash from the lighthouse on Bull Point became visible.

The islands of St. Vincent and St. Antonio are separated from each other by a channel two leagues broad, so I decided to heave to in sight of the St. Antonio light until daybreak.

We got under weigh again at dawn, October 2, and in a few hours were lying at anchor in Porto Grande Bay, St. Vincent. This desolate island, which is an important coaling station and nothing else, inhabited by a robust but ruffianly race of negroes, has been often described; a mere cinder-heap, arid, bare of verdure, almost destitute of water, it is the most dreary, inhospitable-looking place I know, and the volcanic soil seems to soak in the rays of the tropical sun and convert it into a veritable oven at times. But the dismalness of nature is atoned for by the cheeriness and hospitality of one section of the population. For the white community here is almost entirely composed of Englishmen, the staff of the Anglo-Brazilian Telegraph Company—of which this is a very im-portant station—and the employees of the two British coal-kings of the island. Though there had sprung up a new generation of these young fellows since I had visited the island in the "Falcon," yet I met several old friends whose acquaintance I had then made.

Porto Grande, miserable place as it still is, had improved a good deal since I had seen it last. There are hotels here now of a sort, and at one of these on the beach, kept by a pleasant Italian and his Provençal wife, we found it possible to lunch and dine very decently. I notice that I have a tendency in this book to speak of little else save the gastronomic possibilities of the ports I called at in the course of the voyage. But I had visited and described all these places before, and that is some excuse, for the sights were not new to me, whereas a good dinner seems always to have the freshness of novelty. This may sound disgustingly greedy to a sedentary and dyspeptic person; but may I ask whether every sound Britisher does not look upon the quality of his food as one of his most important considerations during his travels abroad. How natural, then, was it that seafarers like ourselves, who were seldom in port and whose diet for months consisted chiefly of tough salt junk and weevily biscuit, should be more vividly impressed by a luxurious meal on shore than by all the lions of these foreign lands.

Here one of the volunteers, our poor old purser, generally known on board as the bellman, left us, and returned to England. The state of his health rendered it unwise for him to proceed further on a voyage of this description.

Suspecting that I might lose others of my crew, I looked round Porto Grande for two fresh paid hands. This is a very bad place to pick up sailors in, but I was lucky in my search. I shipped two young coloured men from the West Indies—one a native of St. Kitt's, and, therefore, an English subject, and the other a Dutchman, hailing from St. Eustatius. These two negroes, whose names were respectively John Joseph Marshall and George Theodosius Spanner, had been loafing about Porto Grande for some time in search of a vessel. The poor fellows had been jumped from a Yankee whaler that had called here.

"Jumping," I may explain, for the benefit of those who do not know the term, is the process by which an unprincipled skipper obtains a crew for nothing. It is done in this way. Hands are shipped, say for a whaling voyage. In time, long arrears of pay are due to the men, as also are their shares in the results of the fishery. But the period for which they have signed articles has not yet been completed, and so they are at the captain's mercy for some time to come. This tyrant, therefore, proceeds to ill-treat them to such an extent that, as soon as a port is reached, they escape on shore and desert the vessel, thereby forfeiting all claim to the money due to them. Thereupon the skipper pockets the earnings of his men, and sails away with a fresh crew, with whom he repeats the process. Some whaling captains are great adepts at jumping, and will even sometimes bully the entire crew into desertion. But those who are not masters of the art dare not risk this, but content themselves with selecting a few hands only, generally those who are weak or unpopular in the forecastle, as victims for their brutality.

John Joseph and Theodosius, as being innocent West Indian blacks, had been the victims of this particular skipper, and nine months' pay was due to them when they deserted. John Joseph shipped with us as cook, Wright being now rated as A. B., while Theodosius served before the mast. They both proved to be excellent fellows.

We found fresh provisions very scarce and dear at Porto Grande. As a rule, tropical fruits and vegetables are plentiful and cheap here, for though St. Vincent is barren, the inner valleys of the neighbouring island of St. Antonio are extremely fertile, and provisions of all sorts, and even fresh water, are brought over from it in the native boats. But smallpox happened now to be very prevalent among the negro population of St. Antonio, so that the island was strictly quarantined, and St. Vincent was cut off from its usual source of supplies.

Our racing spinnaker and its boom had proved to be rather large and unmanageable for the purposes of an ocean voyage; but our balloon foresail was of about the right size for a cruising spinnaker. I accordingly had a small boom made for it here, and it was invariably used for the future in place of the unwieldy racing sail.

From St. Vincent we sailed across the Atlantic to Bahia in Brazil. I had followed exactly the same route with the "Falcon," and found the voyage a tedious one; for, on leaving the region of the north-east trades, a vessel encounters the squally and rainy south-west African monsoons, blowing right in her teeth; and, when these are passed, there lies before one the broad belt of the equatorial doldrums, a region of steaming, debilitating calms, that divides the north-east from the south-east trades.

Under the impression that the log of a small vessel that had made this uncomfortable passage might be of interest to yachting men, I described this portion of the "Falcon's" voyage in my book with more minuteness than usual, with the result that one reviewer characterised the perusal of that particular chapter as being "like eating sawdust." I will profit by this warning, and spare my readers too much log of calms and squalls, doldrums and monsoons, and treat them to as little sawdust as possible.

With the "Falcon" we accomplished the voyage from St. Vincent to Bahia in twenty-two days; but with the "Alerte" we were twenty-six days doing this, for we were not so lucky in our weather, and were delayed by a much longer spell of calms on the line than we had experienced in the "Falcon."

We weighed anchor in the afternoon of October 9 and got out of the harbour under all plain sail. For the first four days we did very well; the wind was south-east and the sea moderate, so that at midday of October 13 we were well on our way, being in latitude 2° 25′ north and longitude 28° 52′ west.

But now our troubles commenced. With a squall the wind shifted to the south-west and we knew that we had reached the dreaded monsoon region. The log was now a record for days of what sailors call dusty weather, and I fear that the reading of it would prove "sawdusty" in the extreme. The south-west monsoon is accompanied by violent thunderstorms, rain, and squalls, and the sea in this portion of the ocean is perpetually confused, so that a vessel turning to windward can make but little progress. Then we came into the abominable region of calms, where we rolled helplessly on the smooth, long swell, while our ropes and sails chafed themselves away with idleness, suffering more wear and tear than they would in a week of gales. Ours was indeed a very unpleasant experience of the doldrums. For some days we made no progress whatever, not even an occasional squall coming down to help us along for a mile or so. In two weeks we only travelled 400 miles, and we did not cross the equator until October 27.

We saw few vessels on this voyage. We spoke two: the French mail steamer "Parana," homeward-bound, and the British ship "Merioneth," of Liverpool, bound south.

We were not only unlucky with our winds but also with our fishing. While crossing this sea on the "Falcon" we had caught quantities of dolphins, thrashers, and kingfish; but on this voyage we caught nothing until we had sighted Fernando Noronha, when we did manage to secure a barracouta and a kingfish.

While rolling about helplessly in the dreary doldrums in the atmosphere of a Turkish bath, there was nothing to interest us save the sunrises and sunsets over the monotonous oil-looking sea. And these for several days in succession were more magnificent than I think I have ever seen before. Sometimes the whole heaven seemed ablaze with flames, and at other times sharply-defined, black, opaque masses of cloud stood out in strange contrast to a background of brilliant and transparent colour, and behind the nearer atmosphere one caught glimpses of vast spreads of the most delicate and tender tints, pink, green, blue and creamy white, looking like a glorious placid ocean of light infinitely far away, studded with ever-changing fairy islands. With the exercise of a very little imagination one could distinguish on that wonderful equatorial sky oceans and continents, mountains of snow and glowing volcanoes, and immense plains of indescribable beauty.

One of the characteristics of the atmosphere of the doldrums is the opaque appearance of the lower banks of clouds. At night they often look like solid black walls close to one; so much so that I was twice called up by our absurd second mate, who had been terrified by the sudden discovery that a large, hitherto unknown island was just under our lee.

We fell in with the south-east trades when we were but two degrees north of the equator; but it was not until we had crossed the line that we were able to record anything like a good run each midday. We were then sailing full and by, on the port tack, and the trades were so high that for three days we were under two reefed mainsail and reefed foresail, the vessel occasionally plunging her bows into the short seas.

At dawn on October 29 we sighted the island of Fernando Noronha on the port bow, and at midday we were close under it. This island, which is about six miles long, presents a beautiful appearance from the sea, with its lofty pinnacles of bare rock towering above the dense green vegetation that covers the hillsides. Fernando Noronha is used as a penal settlement by the Brazilians, and is commanded by a major who has a hundred black troops under him. There are about 1,500 convicts on the island, chiefly blacks and mulattoes; but there is, or recently was, one Englishman among them. It is almost impossible for a prisoner to escape, for there are no boats on the island, and the regulations about landing are very strict; indeed, I believe that no foreign vessel is allowed to hold any communication with the shore, unless in want of water, or other urgent necessity.

On the morning of October 31 we sighted the Brazilian coast near Pernambuco—a long stretch of golden sands beaten by the surf, fringed with waving cocoa-nuts, behind which, far inland, were swelling ranges of forest-clad mountains.

It was a beautiful and very tropical-looking shore, familiar to me, for I had sailed by it on several previous occasions.

We now followed the coast for upwards of 400 miles, observing a distance of five miles off it, so as to be clear of the outlying coral reefs. We passed many of the native fishing catamarans manned by naked negroes, quaint rafts with triangular sails and decks that were under water with every wave.

For three days we coasted along this beautiful land with a favouring wind. On Saturday night, November 2, we opened out the entrance of the Reconcavo or Gulf of Bahia, and, sailing up, we let go our anchor at midnight off the city of

Bahia, close under Fort do Mar, where I had anchored in the
"Falcon."

All my companions were amazed at the beautiful appearance of the city as seen from the sea by night. The churches
and houses of the upper town gleaming like white marble in
the moonlight, with lofty cabbage palms and rank tropical
vegetation growing between, the long lines of well-lit streets
extending for miles round the bay, gave them an idea of the
magnificence of Bahia that a walk through the dirty streets by
daylight on the morrow did much to modify. The old Portuguese city is picturesque but scarcely magnificent.

CHAPTER VIII

BAHIA

ALL hands turned out early on the morning after our arrival anxious for shore-leave, so that they might inspect the city that rose before them so majestically from the edge of the green water. Now could they realise better than by night what a magnificent harbour is this Reconcavo—an extensive inland sea 100 miles in circumference, into which several large rivers pour their waters, surrounded by a country of prodigal fertility, and studded with beautiful islands!

The town was merry as usual with a sound of bells, crackers and rockets. These are never silent in Bahia. It is a most religious city. It is called Bahia dos Todos os Santos, the Bay of All Saints, and every day of the year is the saint's day of some parish or street or even family, and it has to be celebrated by fireworks, which, according to the custom of the country, are let off by day quite as much as by night. If there happened a sudden cessation of this noise of bells, crackers and rockets, I believe the inhabitants would run out of their houses in consternation, under the impression that an earthquake or a revolution had come upon them.

The Bahian custom-house is not open on Sundays; but the authorities were good enough to break through their rule, and, coming off to us in their launch at an early hour, gave us pratique. They also gave us permission to land with our boats at the arsenal, and to put off from it at any hour of the day or night. This important privilege is granted as a matter of courtesy to every foreign man-of-war and yacht. On the other hand, very inconvenient restrictions are placed on merchantmen, originally, I believe, for the purpose of preventing slaves from escaping on board foreign vessels. Slavery has been abolished quite recently, but the old rules still remain in force. No one may leave or board a merchantman after 8 P.M., and any one who is not on the ship's articles cannot do so even in the daytime without a special permit from the custom-house. We were free to do what we pleased during our stay, but I observed that the custom-house boats hovered round the "Alerte" a good deal at night, and that a sharp watch was evidently kept on us. All manual labour is left to the negroes in the Brazils, and a yacht manned for the most part with volunteer milords instead of paid hands must have appeared to the natives an incomprehensible, and consequently a highly suspicious, phenomenon.

Even before we had obtained pratique the energetic ship-chandlers were off to us in their boats, soliciting our custom by shouting to us from a distance. Pratique granted, they closed in upon us. There is a tremendous competition between these gentry at Bahia, as I had discovered while here in the "Falcon." But I was soon recognised, and then all retired from the field save two, between whom the competition waxed most furiously. It seemed that my old ship-chandling firm had split itself into two houses, so the two ex-partners and now bitter rivals boarded the "Alerte," and each claimed me as his own lawful prey.

This was embarrassing, for I had been satisfied with both when they were as one at the time of the "Falcon's" visit; but, as a single ship-chandler at a time is quite enough, I had to make an invidious choice between my old friends. One was an Englishman, the other a Brazilian; so I thought it right to surrender myself into the hands of a fellow-countryman, Mr. Wilson, who carried us off in triumph in his boat as soon as we had donned our shore-going clothes.

We landed at the Praya, the ancient and dirty stone quay which stretches along the shore for four miles, a spot of great commercial activity. Here are the great warehouses whence the coffee, sugar, tobacco, cotton, logwood, and the other produce of this rich tropical land, are shipped to every quarter of the globe. Here, too, are markets of strange fruits and vegetables, and a bazaar where one can buy gorgeous or voluble parrots, baboons and monkeys of many species, pumas and jaguars too, and indeed specimens of nearly all the wild beasts of South America. Grog shops, where poisonous white rum is sold to British seamen, are frequent. Along the quay are ranged the quaint native lighters with their half-naked ebony crews. A jostling, jabbering crowd of negroes and negresses with gaudy robes and turbans throngs the Praya, and when one first lands one is oppressed by a bewildering sense of confusion—a flashing of bright colours—a din of negroes, parrots and monkeys—a compound smell of pineapples and other fruit, of molasses, Africans, bilgewater, tar, filth too of every description; not a monotonous smell, however, but ever varying, now a whiff of hot air sweet with spice, then an odour that might well be the breath of Yellow Jack himself.

There was no yellow fever at the time in Bahia, though it had been rather severe at Rio not long before. We repaired to the ship-chandler's, saw the latest papers and heard all the news. I found that Brazilian politics formed the chief topic of conversation. A stranger visiting this country ten years back would have almost imagined that this was a happy land in which politics were unknown, so little did he hear of them. Now all was changed. Everybody was complaining of the stagnation of business. The Creoles were irritated at the recent abolition of slavery—a measure which, according to them, would ruin the country, but which, in the opinion of some was rendered necessary by the determined resistance of the large bands of fugitive slaves in the southern provinces. The troops were unable to put them down, their success had brought the country to the verge of a general servile insurrection, so that it became merely a question whether the Government should submit quietly to their demands at once or be compelled to do so later on after much bloodshed. I do not think the revolution that took place a few days later was altogether unexpected. There were rumours of it in the air and an uneasy feeling existed among the mercantile classes.

This was my third visit to this port, so I had, of course, plenty of friends in the city. These soon found me out, and I noticed that, despite the supposed unhealthiness of Bahia, none of them looked much the worse for the eight years they had spent here since I had seen them last. There can be no doubt that Brazil enjoys a very healthy climate considering its position within the tropics.

We were elected honorary members of the English Club during our stay at Bahia, and there we found that the object of our voyage had been much discussed. The English papers had advertised us somewhat too well, and though the name of the island we were bound for was not exactly mentioned, my Bahian friends had formed more than a suspicion as to our destination. They, of course, knew that I had visited Trinidad before, and they also were aware that treasure was supposed to be concealed there, for the American adventurer called here after the unsuccessful search to which I have alluded.

"Tell me," said Mr. Wilson, with a smile, when he got me alone, "tell me in confidence. Are you not going to Trinidad again from here?"

When I had replied in the affirmative, he said, "Three years after you sailed from here with the 'Falcon' an American came into my office. He had just come from Trinidad, and was very reserved about it. But two of the crew told me that they had been on shore digging for three days, they did not know what for, but they supposed the captain had some information about hidden treasure. At any rate they found nothing, and while he was at Bahia, the captain seemed to be very disappointed, and would speak of his adventures to no one."

This tallied exactly with the letter of the Danish captain which I have already quoted. It was not altogether agreeable to us to find that our plans were so generally canvassed, for we knew that the Portuguese had laid claim to Trinidad something like two hundred years ago, and it was possible that the Brazilians, as successors to the Portuguese in this quarter of the globe, might consider the island as their own, and assert their right to any valuables we might find upon it. I need scarcely say that I had made up my mind, should we find the treasure, to sail directly to some British port. I would not trust myself in any country of the Spanish or Portuguese; for once in their clutches we should in all probability lose all the results of our labour. The Roman Catholic Church of Spain or Lima might, with a fair show of right, demand the treasure as her own; so might the Governments of Peru, Chile, Brazil, Spain, or Portugal. But if we could once secure it, get it safely home, and divide it, it would be exceedingly difficult for any one to establish a better right to it than we could—for should we not have the right of possession, with nine-tenths of the law on our side?

Bahia is a dull place, but it is an interesting old city, and contains some very picturesque streets, especially those which connect the upper and the lower town, and which wind, in flights of stone steps, up a precipitous wall of rock 240 feet in height. This cliff, despite its steepness, is green with bananas, palms, and other tropical plants, which fill up all the space between the ancient stone-houses and tortuous alleys, producing a very pleasing effect from the sea.

The old Dutch and Portuguese houses are very solidly built of stone, and among them are some of the most ancient buildings of the New World. The Fort la Mar, under which we were anchored, is a picturesque fortress constructed by the Dutch 400 years ago on a rocky islet in the harbour. The cathedral and some other of the ecclesiastical buildings in the upper town are built of marble that was brought from Europe. In the olden days—and to some extent this is the case even now—everything needed by the Spanish and Portuguese colonists of the New World, with the exception of gold and jewels, was imported to them from the mother-countries. Thus there are cities in the heart of South America which have quarries of marble in their immediate vicinity, and whose churches are, notwithstanding, built of marble blocks carried from Europe by sea and land at tremendous cost. With its vast arable lands, that might supply the granaries of the world, the River Plate district, until quite recently, depended on foreign countries for its supplies of grain. The old theory of the Conquistadores, that it was beneath their dignity to perform any labour save that of extracting gold from the country and its natives, seems never to have been quite eradicated from the Creole mind.

I could see few changes in Bahia since my last visit. It seemed the same busy, dirty, old place. A new broad carriage-road had been carried up the cliff, and this, together with the hydraulic lift which connects the lower with the upper town, has certainly diminished the number of sedan chairs. Once these were a quaint feature in a Bahian street scene. They are almost of the same model as those in use in London 200 years ago, and are carried by stout negroes. Now they are only employed by Creole ladies of the old school, who do not care to sit in the trams by the side of their late slaves.

The crew of the "Alerte" had now the opportunity of relaxing themselves a little before sailing away for the scene of their real work. Some made expeditions up the rivers into the beautiful country that surrounds Bahia, and the frequent race-meetings afforded amusement to others. I believe we were lucky, on the whole, while matching ourselves against the local bookmaker, and realised a few thousands—not of pounds, but reis, of which a thousand are equivalent to two shillings.

Our first and second mate left us after we had been a few days at Bahia, packing up their traps and getting ashore before they ventured to announce their intention. From this date things went smoother with us. The cause of all the mischief on board had departed. There was an alacrity and cheerfulness fore and aft that had been wanting so far. Now when reefing or other work had to be done it was accomplished by a third of the number of hands, in one-third of the time and with none of the fuss that seemed to be necessary before. I do not go so far as to say that a sort of millennium came to the "Alerte"—there was still, of course, occasional discord, but on what vessel are there not rows and growlings? It can be safely asserted, however, that from the time we left Bahia the "Alerte" was far freer than the average foreign-going vessel from troubles of this description; and this is very creditable seeing that our crew was so unusually constituted, half of the men being paying, instead of paid, hands, and, therefore, possibly inclined to imagine that they had a right to more voice in the management of things than was quite feasible.

The crew of the "Alerte" now consisted of ten all told:—Dr. Cloete-Smith, Mr. Pollock, Mr. Powell, Mr. Purssell, and myself aft; Ted Milner, John Wright, Arthur Cotton, and the two coloured men forward. Of the nine volunteers who sailed from England five thus remained.

None of the gentlemen above mentioned had any practical knowledge of the sea when we left Southampton; but they picked up a good deal in the course of the voyage to Bahia, and now set to with a will to learn more. I was the only navigator on board when we sailed from Bahia, but before the cruise was over everybody aft could take his observations of the sun and work out his latitude and longitude. I now appointed Dr. Cloete-Smith as my mate, he to take the port watch and myself the starboard. Mr. Pollock and Mr. Purssell undertook the posts of purser and carpenter.

We laid in a quantity of provisions at Bahia; these, in consequence partly of the heavy duties and partly of the constant obstacles placed by a corrupt administration in the way of all commerce, are excessively dear in this port. Among other stores we procured two barrels of salt beef, which proved to be somewhat better than we got at Santa Cruz, a cask of rough and strong Portuguese wine, cases of preserved guavas, tamarinds, and figs; and, of course, as many pineapples, hands of bananas, oranges, yams, sweet potatoes, and pumpkins as we could carry.

Here, too, we purchased some tools, a large iron cooking-pot for our camp on the island, some blasting powder, and several stout bamboos for the purpose of constructing rafts.

We had had enough of Bahia in a week and were all ready for sea again on November 9; but as several letters expected by members of the expedition had not arrived, we put off our departure until the coming of the next mail steamer from England. It was lucky for us that we did this, for we thereby escaped some rather tempestuous weather.

On November 11 the Royal Mail steamer "La Plata" arrived from the north, bringing with her the missing letters. We had intended to sail at daybreak on the following morning, but the glass began to fall and the wind rose in the night. In the morning the sky had a very stormy appearance and a fresh south-west gale was blowing. On the following day—

November 13—there was a continuance of the same weather, and the scud overhead was travelling at a great rate.

An English cargo steamer came in this day from the southward, so I went on shore to find her captain and enquire from him what it was like outside the bay. He told me that he had been overtaken by the gale in the latitude of Cape Frio, and that a heavy sea was running in the Atlantic, while on the bar the breakers would be dangerous for a small vessel. Hearing this, impatient as we were to get away, I decided that it would be better to remain where we were until the gale had blown itself out.

This was, no doubt, the fag-end of a *pampero* or River Plate hurricane. The *pampero*—so called because, after rising in the Andes, it sweeps over the vast plains of the *pampas*, increasing in force as it travels—blows with great fury at the mouth of the River Plate and sometimes extends far north. I had had some experience of *pamperos* and was not fond of them. I rode out one on the "Falcon" at anchor off Montevideo, and on that occasion fifteen solid stone houses were blown down in a row on the sea front, the exhibition building at Buenos Ayres was destroyed, and a barque lying at anchor near us was capsized by the first gust. We ran before another of these storms for three days and were nearly lost.

The *pampero* was our bugbear while we lay off Trinidad; for this islet is within the range of the more formidable of these gales, and, even when they do not extend so far, the great swell raised by them rolls up hundreds of miles to the northward of the wind's influence and breaks furiously all around the exposed shores of Trinidad.

Towards evening the wind moderated and the glass began to rise, but the rain continued to fall heavily. On the following morning, November 14, the weather had still further improved; so anchor was weighed at 8 A.M. and we sailed out of the harbour, my companions in very cheerful spirits and eager to get to the desert island and be at work with pick and shovel as soon as possible.

We had now done with civilisation for some time to come, and we had no idea when and where, and under what conditions, we should next see any men save those forming our own little band.

Trinidad is roughly 680 nautic miles from Bahia; we sighted it in exactly six days from the time we weighed anchor.

The experiences of our first day out did not promise well for a smart voyage. We tumbled about a good deal on the bar at the mouth of the bay, and found that the sea outside had not yet gone down. The wind was moderate and variable, but generally south-east—that is, right in our teeth. We tacked ship three times in the course of the day, and made little progress against the head sea.

On the following day, November 15, things looked better; the wind veered to the eastward, so that the yacht could lay her course with her sheets slacked off a bit.

The next day the wind was fairer still—from the east-north-east—blowing fresh, and raising a steep, confused sea, for the south-west swell of the *pampero* had not yet entirely subsided. We close-reefed the foresail so as to prevent the vessel driving her nose into the seas, and during this day and the next, November 17, we were constantly tricing up the tack of the mainsail in the squalls.

On the 18th and 19th the wind was moderate, so we had all canvas on the old vessel again, including topsail and balloon foresail; and on the morning of November 20 all hands were in eager expectance of catching the first glimpse of Treasure Island.

At about 8 A.M. it suddenly appeared right ahead, a faint blue peak on the horizon, fully forty miles away.

CHAPTER IX

TREASURE ISLAND AT LAST

WE sailed on towards the desert island under all canvas, but did not reach it for eight hours from the time we first sighted it.

As we neared it, the features of this extraordinary place could gradually be distinguished. The north side, that which faced us, is the most barren and desolate portion of the island, and appears to be utterly inaccessible. Here the mountains rise sheer from the boiling surf—fantastically shaped of volcanic rock; cloven by frightful ravines; lowering in perpendicular precipices; in places overhanging threateningly, and, where the mountains have been shaken to pieces by the fires and earthquakes of volcanic action, huge landslips slope steeply into the yawning ravines—landslips of black and red volcanic *débris*, and loose rocks large as houses, ready on the slightest disturbance to roll down, crashing, into the abysses below. On the summit of the island there floats almost constantly, even on the clearest day, a wreath of dense vapour, never still, but rolling and twisting into strange shapes as the wind eddies among the crags. And above this cloud-wreath rise mighty pinnacles of coal-black rock, like the spires of some gigantic Gothic cathedral piercing the blue southern sky.

The loftiest peak is about three thousand feet above the sea, but on account of the extreme precipitousness of the island it appears much higher.

As a consequence of the recoil of the rollers from the shore we found that, as we got nearer in, the ocean swell under us increased in height, and rose and fell in an uneasy confused fashion. The breakers were dashing up the cliffs with an ominous roar, showing us that, in all probability, landing would be out of the question for the present.

We passed North Point and opened out North-west Bay. At the further end of the bay we saw before us the Monument, or Ninepin, as it is called on the charts—a stupendous pinnacle

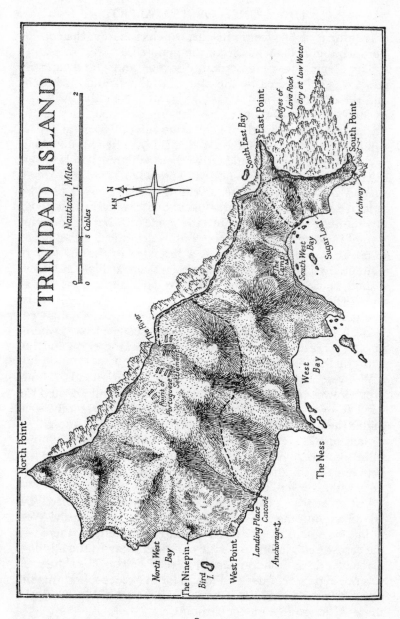

TRINIDAD ISLAND

Nautical Miles

North Point

North West Bay

The Ninepin

Bird I.

West Point

Landing Place
Cascade

Anchorage

The Ness

West Bay

The River

Point of
Portuguese Settlement

The Cliffs

South West Bay

Sugar Loaf

South East Bay

East Point

Ledges of
Lava Rock

dry at low water

South Point

Archway

85

of basaltic rock 850 feet in height, which rises from the edge of the surf, and is detached from the main cliffs.

The scenery was indescribably savage and grand, and its effect was heightened by the roaring of the surf on the beach, and the echoes of it in the ravines, as well as by the shrill and melancholy cries of thousands of sea-birds so unaccustomed to the presence of man that they came off the crags and flew round us in evident wonder as we sailed by, often approaching so close to us that we could strike them with our hands.

My companions had expected, from what I had told them, to find this islet a strange, uncanny place, barren, torn by volcanic action and generally forbidding, and now they gazed at the shore with amazement, and confessed that my description of its scenery was anything but exaggerated. It would be impossible to convey in words a just idea of the mystery of Trinidad. The very colouring seems unearthly—in places dismal black, and in others the fire-consumed crags are of strange metallic hues, vermilion red and copper yellow. When one lands on its shores this uncanny impression is enhanced. It bears all the appearance of being an accursed spot, whereupon no creatures can live, save the hideous land-crabs and foul and cruel sea-birds.

We were now coasting under the lee of the island and our progress was but slow, for the high mountains intercepted the wind from us, and we were often becalmed on the oily swell under the hottest sun we had yet experienced. Occasionally a violent squall, but of short duration, would sweep down on us from some ravine and help us along. What wind there was between the squalls came from every point of the compass in turns, and we were constantly taken aback.

But at last we passed the rocky islet which I named Bird Island at the time of my former visit, and, doubling the West Point, we entered a bay which I recognised well, for there was the cascade still falling over the cliff, and, near it, the landing-place off which I had anchored in the "Falcon." As the swell was not high here, I decided to anchor at once; so, bringing the vessel as near in as was prudent—about six cables from the shore—I let go in eighteen fathoms.

The scene before us was a fine one. A very steep and rugged ravine clove the mountain from summit to base. At the bottom of this ravine a stream fell in a cascade over a ledge of black rock on to the beach, about thirty feet below. One could trace the silver line of the falling water in many other parts of the ravine, especially in one place far up, where it fell over a gigantic black precipice.

The mountain-sides were barren, save in spots where a coarse grass grew sparsely. At the very head of the ravine were downs beautifuly green, with a dense grove of trees, the nature of which it was not easy to distinguish from so far below; but, as I had ascended this ravine during my last visit to Trinidad, I knew that these were tree-ferns, which only grow on this portion of the island high up among the damp clouds, and are in charming contrast to the desolation that prevails around them.

Between the foot of the mountains and the surf extends a narrow beach of rugged stones of all sizes fallen from above, and the black heads of rocks appear here and there in the middle of the surf, so that any attempt at landing seems a risky venture.

But I knew where the safe landing-place was, and soon recognised it again, though it was not to be easily distinguished from the vessel. I pointed it out to my companions. Some forty yards to the left of the cascade an irregularly shaped rocky ledge extends from the beach some way out into the deep water beyond the beach, and thus forms a natural pier. I had often found it quite an easy matter to land here when to do so anywhere else would be impossible; for, as a rule, the seas do not break until they have rolled some way inside the end of this point; so that, by approaching it carefully, and waiting till the boat is on the summit of a wave and near the level of the top of the rock, one can leap or scramble on to it with the exercise of a little agility. There are occasions, however, when the seas wash right over this ledge.

Looking from our anchorage we could see the coast as far as West Point on one side of us, with the head of the Ninepin just visible above the cape; and on the other side as far as the promontory of basaltic columns which forms the western extremity of West Bay, and which I have named The Ness on my plan of the island.

As soon as the sails were stowed I went below with the doctor to talk over our immediate plans. It was now five in the evening, so it was too late to attempt a landing, even if the conditions were favourable, which they were not; for every now and again a sea would break over the pier, sending showers of spray high into the air.

While we were discussing things, there suddenly came a violent thumping on the deck above us, and from the shouts and laughter of the men we knew that something exciting was going on; so we went up the companion-ladder to see what the fun might be. We found that a fair-sized shark was tumbling about the deck in very active fashion, while Ted was dodging him, knife in hand, ready to give him his *coup de grâce*. Our sportsman had got his lines out as soon as all had been made snug on deck, but his sport for the first hour consisted of nothing but sharks, of which he caught several. After this he had better luck and was able to supply the cook with fish enough for dinner and breakfast for all hands.

The sea round Trinidad swarms with fish; but, for some reason, though we got as many as we required, they were not to be so readily caught now as at the time of my first visit; for then we hauled them in as fast as we could drop our hooks in the water.

There are various species of edible fish here; among others, dolphins, rock-cod, hind-fish, black-fish, and pig-fish. None of these hot-water-fish are to be compared in flavour to those of Europe, and we found that the sharks were the least insipid of the lot; stewed shark and onions is not a dish to be despised.

The accompanying plan of Trinidad is copied from the chart of the South Atlantic, which I made use of on this voyage, but contains some additions and corrections of my own, to which allusion will be made in the proper place. It will be seen that, according to this plan, the island is rather more than five miles long. Another chart which I possess gives its length as only three miles, which I am sure is wrong; but, on the other hand, this last chart is the most correct in some other respects, and marks outlying shoals which are not indicated on the other. There are, indeed, no absolutely reliable charts of this island; for the different surveys have been somewhat cursory, and each has repeated the faults of its predecessors. The longitude has, I believe, never been accurately determined, and even the latitude of the landing-place is, if I am not much mistaken, more than a mile out on the chart.

However, the plan which I have copied is sufficiently correct to illustrate all that I have to say concerning our work and exploration on Trinidad, and, before going further with the narrative, it will be well to enter into some explanation of the task that was before us.

The treasure was supposed to be hidden in South-west Bay, in the little ravine which I have indicated on the plan just to the left of our camp.

It will be observed that the yacht was anchored out of sight of this spot, and at a distance of two and a half miles from it as the crow flies. My companions were, I imagine, somewhat surprised at this manœuvre of mine, especially when I told them that it was highly improbable that we should shift our anchorage any nearer to the scene of our operations on shore. Later on, however, they realised that there was a good reason for the course I had taken.

My former experiences off Trinidad with the "Falcon" had convinced me that the anchorage off the cascade was far the safest, indeed that here only could one remain at all for any length of time. It must be remembered that a vessel is never really secure when anchored off a small oceanic island like Trinidad. One should be always prepared to slip one's anchor and be off to sea at once should it come on to blow. It is, therefore, necessary to lie at some distance from the land, so as to have plenty of room to get away on either tack. If one is too near the shore one incurs great risk, as I frequently discovered while coasting later on; for even though it be blowing hard outside, one is becalmed under the cliffs or subjected to shifting flaws and whirlwinds, so that the vessel becomes unmanageable, and is driven straight on to the fatal rocks by the send of the swell. I need scarcely say that to come in contact with this shore, even in the finest weather, would involve the certain destruction of any craft in a very few seconds.

The anchorage off the cascade possesses many advantages. The coast here is free from any outlying dangers, and there is a depth of five fathoms close to the beach. One cannot be embayed here, for the coast beyond West Point trends away northward almost at right angles to the south-west shore, so that from the anchorage it is easy to get away on either tack, according to the direction of the wind. Here, too, the sea is smoother than anywhere else, except on rare occasions, for the prevailing winds are north-east to south-east, more generally south-east.

Now, the only other possible anchorage for us would have been in South-west Bay, in very convenient proximity to our camp; but this, though it might do for a day or two, was absolutely unfitted for a lengthy stay, more especially as difficulties might occur with the vessel while I was on shore myself and only inexperienced people were in charge of her. In this bay one is surrounded by dangers. South Point is on one side, with the current generally setting directly on to it and across the perilous shoals that extend a mile and a half seaward. On the other side is the cape dividing West and South-west Bays, off which also lie several dangerous islets and rocks. According to the Admiralty chart South-west Bay itself is quite clean, with a uniform depth of ten fathoms. As a matter of fact, it is full of sunken rocks, and there is an island right in the middle of it, the position of which I have shown in plan; its existence is ignored by all the charts. Surrounded as the bay is by lofty mountains, the winds are very uncertain within it, so that if one should have to weigh anchor it might be difficult to extricate the vessel from her dangerous position even by the exercise of the smartest seamanship. Lastly, it affords no shelter from the prevailing wind, south-east, which often raises a nasty sea, and, what is more, it is entirely exposed to the storm-wind of these seas, the dreaded *pampero*, which blows right into it. Any one in charge of a vessel brought up in this trap would be compelled to get under weigh frequently under most difficult circumstances, and would live an unenviable life of perpetual anxiety. This information will, I trust, be of use to any fresh adventurers who propose to hunt for the treasure of Trinidad.

Though I would not venture into South-west Bay with the yacht, I knew that we should have to carry our stores and tools there by boat and land them on the beach opposite to the treasure ravine; for to transport them by land from the easy landing-place near the cascade would be an almost impossible undertaking.

According to the dead pirate's statement, he and his comrades had surveyed South-west Bay and discovered the best channel between the rocks. He gave the directions for finding this channel to Captain P——, and its existence had been verified by both the South Shields explorers; but as they had brought back an alarming account of its dangers, and boats had been lost in it, I considered that it would be a wise precaution for me to land at the pier in the first place, walk—or rather crawl and climb, for there is not much walking to be done on that journey—across the island and survey South-west Bay from the hills above it, before attempting to beach a boat there.

In the evening we held a council in the saloon over our pipes and I explained my plans for the following day.

I had explored the island pretty thoroughly while here before and I knew that it mainly consisted of inaccessible peaks and precipices, among which there were very few passes practicable for men. In many places the cliffs fall precipitously into the sea, affording no foothold. I had landed in both North-west Bay and the bay beyond it, and, though there were sandy beaches in both these, still, one could go on further, for sheer promontories on either side and mountains equally insurmountable at the back cut off all communication between these coves and the rest of the island. I also knew that it would be impossible for me to walk along the beach from the pier to South-west Bay, for between these were the two capes that bound West Bay, both opposing barriers of precipices to one's advance.

But while here with the "Falcon," after a difficult and dangerous search which has been fully described in the narrative of that voyage, I at last discovered a pass, and I believe it is the only one, by which the mountains at the centre of the island can be traversed and the windward shore attained.

First, I ascended the steep ravine down which the cascade flows. Having arrived at the summit of the ravine I crossed the groves of tree-ferns, and, after making several descents into ravines which terminated in precipices and so compelled me to retrace my steps, I succeeded in discovering a gully which led me to the beach on the north-east side of the island. From here I found it possible to walk along the beach to South Point, for no insurmountable capes intervened; and from South-east Bay there was an easy pass under the Sugarloaf Mountain by which the Treasure bay could be reached. This was the journey which I intended to make once again on the following morning. This route, together with others taken in the course of our explorations, are indicated with dotted lines on the plan of Trinidad in this book, and I believe that they are the only accessible ways on the island.

I knew by experience that the passage over the mountains to the windward beach was both arduous and perilous, and that to climb to South-west Bay, survey it, and return to the pier would occupy the best part of three days.

The doctor volunteered to accompany me, and I decided to take him with me. It was indeed important that he should make himself acquainted with the pass; for it had been settled that whenever I remained with the yacht he should be in command of the party working on shore, and, as the only reliable water-supply I knew of was at the cascade, it might become necessary for him to lead the men across the mountains to it should a water-famine occur at South-west Bay. Again, it was certain that bad weather would occasionally make the landing of boats at South-west Bay impossible for weeks at a time, so that, if there were some urgent reason for communicating with the yacht, this could only be done by crossing to the pier landing-place, at which I am of opinion that one can land ten times with safety to once in South-west Bay. It had been my intention to form a depôt of stores at the pier, but this we found to be unnecessary.

After I had made the above explanations to my companions assembled in the saloon, our sportsman, who had been listening attentively, remarked: "Skipper, you have given us plenty of reasons for taking Cloete-Smith with you to-morrow and teaching him the roads; but you have omitted the most important reason of all. Let me inform you that you won't get us to do any work on shore on Sundays; so on every Sunday afternoon we will put on our best clothes, and the doctor will have to take us over the pass to the pier, where we can do a sort of church-parade and listen to the band. I suppose there will be a bar there, too, with Theodosius as barman presiding over the rum-barrel."

CHAPTER X

THE SUMMIT OF TRINIDAD

ON the following morning—November 21—as soon as breakfast was over, the doctor and myself started for the shore. In view of the rough climbing before us we did not burden ourselves with much baggage, but set forth in light marching order. We dispensed with blankets, and, in addition to the somewhat scanty clothing we had on, we carried merely provisions for three days, consisting of some ship's biscuit, a few strips of Brazilian *charki* or jerked beef—rather rank—some dried figs, a flask of rum, a tin bottle to hold water, one pannikin, tobacco, pipes, and matches.

We could see from the deck that there was considerable surf on the beach, and it was evident that we should not find the landing at the pier to be so easy a matter as it often is.

Two of the paid hands pulled us off in the dinghy. When we were about half-way to the shore we perceived a bright red object on an eminence near the cascade. On getting nearer we distinguished this to be a ragged red flag flying from a pole. This was a startling discovery for us, and might signify that some rival expedition had landed on the island.

We reached the pier and found a high swell rolling by it, while eddies and overfalls round the outer end of it caused the boat to become more or less unmanageable, driving her first in one direction, then in another, so that she could not be brought very close to, without risk of staving her in against the rocks.

Under these circumstances the only safe method of getting on shore was to jump into the water. The boat was backed in towards the pier end, the men pulling a few strokes ahead whenever a wave threatened to dash her on to it. I stood in the stern and awaited a favourable opportunity, then jumped overboard and clambered quickly up the pier side before the

94

next roller should wash me off. Then the boat was backed in again, and the doctor repeated the performance.

We had no particular objection to the wetting we had received, but a good many of our biscuits were converted into a pulp and our figs were pickled with the sea-water.

So here we were at last safely on shore at Trinidad, both in high spirits at the prospect before us, for we were eager to commence the exploration that might result in who could tell what magnificent results.

Climbing over the rugged top of the pier we descended on the beach, which at high water is partly overflowed, the pier being then converted into an island. We scrambled over the rocks and scoriæ to the height by the cascade on which the flag was, and then our suspicions were put at rest by what we discovered. A good-sized barrel had been firmly jammed between the rocks in a prominent place and filled with stones. A pole had been planted in the barrel, and from this floated the red flag we had seen. It was in so ragged a condition that it was impossible to say whether it had ever been a British flag or not. Under it was a wooden tablet, on which was painted the following inscription: "H.M.S. 'Ruby,' February 26, 1889." There was also a bottle on the cask containing the cards of the commander of the vessel, Captain Kennedy, and his wardroom officers.

Having thus satisfied ourselves that no enemy was in possession of the island, we went to the cascade. This stream rises among the tree-ferns at the summit of the mountain and rushes down the gully with a considerable volume of water. This issue is, I should imagine, perennial.

Then we commenced our ascent, which involved no light work. The gully was excessively steep. We were climbing up a staircase of great rocks, and often where there were insurmountable precipices we had to make a *detour* round the mountain-side, creeping carefully along the steep declivities that overhung the cliffs, the rock and earth crumbling beneath our feet as we went; for one of the most unpleasant peculiarities of this island is that it is nowhere solid; it is rotten throughout, its substance has been disintegrated by volcanic fires and by the action of water, so that it is everywhere tumbling to pieces. As one travels over the mountains one is ever starting miniature landslips and dislodging great stones, which roll, thundering, down the cliffs, gathering other companions as they go until a very avalanche is formed. On this day the doctor, who was a little ahead of me at the time, sent adrift a stone weighing a hundredweight at the least, which just cleared my head as I stooped down to dodge it. We were on a dangerous part of the mountain, and had it struck me it must have impelled me over a precipice several hundred feet in height. After this we followed parallel tracks wherever this was feasible.

This unstableness of Trinidad causes a perpetual sense of insecurity while one is on the mountains. One knows not when some overhanging pinnacle may topple down. One great source of danger is that there are many declivities which can be descended but not ascended, and it would be easy to get hopelessly imprisoned at the foot of one of these. In the "Cruise of the 'Falcon'" is described one really terrible experience we went through. Our exploring party had found no water, and the boy was practically dying of thirst. So, driven by urgent necessity—for we saw by the configuration of the mountains that we should almost certainly find water at the bottom of a certain ravine—we proceeded to descend to it down a great slope, not of loose *débris*, but of half-consolidated volcanic matter like half-baked bricks, and very brittle. This slope became steeper as we advanced and very dangerous, but it was impossible to retrace our steps. When we attempted to ascend, the mountain slid away under our feet, crumbling into ashes. It was like climbing a treadmill. So we had to abandon this hope and go still further down, lying on our backs, progressing inch by inch carefully, one of us occasionally sliding down a few yards and sending an avalanche before him. We knew not to the edge of what precipices this dreadful way would lead us. Luckily we reached the bottom in safety and found water.

I determined not to get into any difficulties of this description in the course of our present journey.

We gradually ascended the ravine, sometimes climbing on

one side of it, sometimes on the other, and occasionally wading through the water at the bottom, according to which route was the safest.

The nature of the scenery around us was now grand in the extreme, and had a weird character of its own that I have never perceived on other mountains. The jagged and torn peaks, the profound chasms, the huge landslips of black rocks, the slopes of red volcanic ash destitute of vegetation, in themselves produce a sense of extreme desolation; but this is heightened by the presence of a ghastly dead vegetation and by the numberless uncanny birds and land-crabs which cover all the rocks.

This lonely islet is perhaps the principal breeding place for sea-birds in the south Atlantic. Here multitudes of man-of-war birds, gannets, boobies, cormorants, and petrels have their undisturbed haunts. Not knowing how dangerous he is, they treat their superior animal, man, with a shocking want of due respect. The large birds more especially attack one furiously if one approaches their nests in the breeding season, and in places where one has to clamber with hands as well as feet, and is therefore helpless, they are positively dangerous.

As for the land-crabs, which are unlike any I have seen elsewhere, they swarm all over the island in incredible numbers. I have even seen them two or three deep in shady places under the rocks; they crawl over everything, polluting every stream, devouring anything—a loathsome lot of brutes, which were of use, however, round our camp as scavengers. They have hard shells of a bright saffron colour, and their faces have a most cynical and diabolic expression. As one approaches them they stand on their hind legs and wave their pincers threateningly, while they roll their hideous goggle eyes at one in a dreadful manner. If a man is sleeping or sitting down quietly these creatures will come up to have a bite at him, and would devour him if he was unable for some reason to shake them off; but we murdered so many in the vicinity of our camp during our stay on the island, that they certainly became less bold, and it seemed almost as if the word had been passed all over Trinidad that we were dangerous animals, to be shunned

97

by every prudent crab. Even when we were exploring remote districts we at last found that they fled in terror, instead of menacing us with their claws.

But the great mystery of this mysterious island is the forest of dead trees which covers it and which astonishes every visitor.

The following account of this wood is taken from the "Cruise of the 'Falcon'" and as it was nine years ago, so is it now:—

"What struck us as remarkable was, that though in this cove there was no live vegetation of any kind, there were traces of an abundant extinct vegetation. The mountain slopes were thickly covered with dead wood—wood, too, that had evidently long since been dead; some of these leafless trunks were prostrate, some still stood up as they had grown. . . . When we afterwards discovered that over the whole of this extensive island, from the beach up to the summit of the highest mountain—at the bottom and on the slopes of every now barren ravine, on whose loose-rolling stones no vegetation could possible take root—these dead trees were strewed so closely as it is possible for trees to grow; and when we further perceived that they all seemed to have died at one and the same time, as if plague-struck, and that no single live specimen, young or old, was to be found anywhere—our amazement was increased."

"At one time Trinidad must have been covered with one magnificent forest, presenting to passing vessels a far different appearance to that it now does, with its inhospitable and barren crags."

"The descriptions given in the 'Directory' allude to these forests; therefore, whatever catastrophe it may have been that killed off all the vegetation of the island, it must have occurred within the memory of man."

"Looking at the rotten, broken-up condition of the rock, and the nature of the soil, where there is a soil—a loose powder, not consolidated like earth, but having the appearance of fallen volcanic ash—I could not help imagining that some great eruption had brought about all this desolation; Trinidad is the acknowledged centre of a small volcanic patch that lies in this portion of the South Atlantic, therefore I think this theory a more probable one than that of a long drought, a not very likely contingency in this rather rainy region."

Some time after the publication of the "Cruise of the 'Falcon' " I came across an excellent description of Trinidad in Captain Marryat's novel, "Frank Mildmay." It is obvious from the following passage, which I quote from that work, that the trees had been long dead at the date of its publication, 1829:—

"Here a wonderful and most melancholy phenomenon arrested our attention. Thousands and thousands of trees covered the valley, each of them about thirty feet high; but every tree was dead, and extended its leafless boughs to another—a forest of desolation, as if nature had at some particular moment ceased to vegetate! There was no underwood or grass. On the lowest of the dead boughs, the gannets, and other sea-birds, had built their nests, in numbers uncountable. Their tameness, as Cowper says, 'was shocking to me.' So unaccustomed did they seem to man that the mothers brooding over their young only opened their beaks, in a menacing attitude, at us as we passed by them. How to account satisfactorily for the simultaneous destruction of this vast forest of trees was very difficult; there was no want of rich earth for nourishment of the roots. The most probable cause appeared to me a sudden and continued eruption of sulphuric effluvia from the volcano; or else by some unusually heavy gale of wind or hurricane the trees had been drenched with salt water to their roots. One or the other of these causes must have produced the effect. The philosopher or the geologist must decide."

Captain Marryat was evidently unaware that these dead trees are to be found on the heights 3,000 feet above the sea-level, as well as in the valleys, or he would not have suggested salt water as the cause of their destruction.

His description proves that the trees were dead at least sixty years ago, and in all probability they had been dead for a long time before. The latest record I have been able to discover which describes live trees as existing on Trinidad is dated as far back as 1700. The Ninepin and the Sugarloaf, now utterly barren, were then crowded with trees of a great size.

Though some of this timber is rotten, a large proportion of it is not decayed in the least, but when cut with the axe presents the appearance of a sound, well-seasoned wood. It is gnarled and knotty, extremely hard and heavy, its specific gravity being but slightly less than that of water. It is of a dark reddish colour and of very close grain.

I brought a log of it home and sent it to a cabinet-maker, who found that it would take an excellent polish. On sending this specimen to Kew I was informed that the wood "probably belongs to the family Myrtaceæ, and possibly to the species Eugenia." I find that this species includes the pimento or allspice, the rose-apple and other aromatic and fruit-producing trees; so that desert Trinidad may at one time have been a delicious spice-island.

The doctor and myself toiled on up the gully, whose slopes, as we approached the summit, became less rugged, and here the ferns grew up between the trunks of the dead trees, spreading wide their beautiful fronds of fresh green.

When we had come to a spot a little below the source of the stream we left the gully—not before we had drunk our fill and replenished the bottle—and ascended the down where the tree-ferns grow thickest. The soil is here very loose and presents the appearance of having been quite recently ploughed up, while it is honeycombed with the holes of the teeming land-crabs.

Soon we reached the summit of the plateau, where a pleasant breeze stirred the ferns and we could now command a magnificent view not only over the mountains we had climbed but over the weather side of the island as well. I remembered the scene, for I had looked down from here nine years before. On the weather side of the island the mountains are even more precipitous than on the lee side, but on the other hand they do not run sheer into the sea, for at their base extend great green slopes continued by broad sandy beaches. Along all this coast are shallow flats and outlying rocks on which the surf breaks perpetually. Thirty miles out to sea rise the inaccessible rocky islets of Martin Vas.

The plateau we were on was covered with a luxuriant vegetation, for in addition to the tree-ferns there were large bushes of some species of acacia, a tall thorny plant with flowers like those of scarlet-runners and bearing large beans, flowering grasses, and various other plants. I collected specimens of these later on, which were lost, however, with other stores shortly before we abandoned the island, in consequence of the capsizing of our boat while launching her in Treasure Bay.

It seemed strange to find so beautiful a garden, high up, almost unapproachable for the perils that surround it, throned as it is on a wilderness of rock rising up to it in chaotic masses and sheer precipices from the shore far below. The sailors under Frank Mildmay discovered this grove before me. In all his descriptions of places and scenery Captain Marryat is singularly faithful to the truth, even in the minutest details. In this respect indeed he is more conscientious in his works of fiction than are most travellers in their presumedly true narratives. The most minute and accurate description of Trinidad that I have come across is in "Frank Mildmay," and it is easy to identify every spot mentioned in that book. The author must himself have visited this strange place, and his imagination was strongly stirred by it. He gives us graphic pictures of "the ironbound coast with high and pointed rocks, frowning defiance over the unappeasable and furious waves which break incessantly at their feet." His hero also experiences the usual difficulty in landing; men and boat are nearly lost, and in all his thrilling narrative there is not the least exaggeration. All the events described might well have happened, and probably did happen.

Of the grove he says:—"The men reported that they had gained the summit of the mountain, where they had discovered a large plain, skirted by a species of fern-tree from twelve to eighteen feet high—that on this plain they had seen a herd of goats; and among them could distinguish one of enormous size which appeared to be their leader. They also found many wild hogs."

We saw no goats or hogs and I am confident that none are now left alive. We did, however, in the course of our digging discover what appeared to be the bones of a goat. It is well known that these animals once abounded here. Captain Halley, of the "Paramore Pink," afterwards Dr. Halley, Astronomer-Royal, landed on this island April 17, 1700, and put on it some goats and hogs for breeding, as also a pair of guinea-fowl which he carried from St. Helena. "I took," says his journal, "possession of the island in his Majesty's name, as knowing it to be granted by the King's letters-patent, leaving the Union Jack flying."

The American commander, Amaso Delano, visited Trinidad in 1803. He writes:—"We found plenty of goats and hogs. We saw some cats, and these three sorts of quadrupeds were the only animals we saw on the island."

Possibly the land-crabs have gobbled all these up, for the only quadrupeds we came across were mice.

Having attained the summit of the island the doctor and myself took a rest under the shade of the tree-ferns, while we partook of a frugal lunch of biscuits and rum, the indispensable pipes, of course, following.

CHAPTER XI

ON THE ROAD TO TREASURE BAY

HAVING smoked our pipes we continued our journey. At first I was a very sanguine guide. I thought I should have no difficulty in recognising the ravine by which, nine years before, I had descended to the windward shore. But in this I was mistaken, for I found it extremely difficult to find my way to it again.

At any rate we were not now about to undergo the great toil, thirst and danger that I had experienced during my former visit, for I at least knew some of the places to avoid, and this was a matter of importance. As we clambered along the edges of the mountains, looking for the pass, I was able to condemn at once as false passages several promising-looking routes, the vain trial of which had exhausted myself and my companions on my previous expedition.

For instance, there was one long slope of volcanic *débris* of a ruddy colour which appeared from where we stood to join on to the green hills below and so to lead to the sandy beaches. The doctor was anxious to attempt this easy-looking way, but I knew the deceitful place too well of old. It tempts one further and further down, ever getting steeper, until one suddenly finds oneself at the edge of a frightful precipice, invisible from above, which compels one at great risk to retrace one's painful steps to the heights.

In the course of my first exploration we made so many false descents of these ravines and slopes, all terminating in precipices and driving us back again, that at last, finding no water, we were completely worn out and nearly perished of thirst. The heat is intense on Trinidad, especially at this season of the year, when the sun is vertical, and to climb these hot crags through the suffocating air is the most completely exhausting work I have ever undertaken. No other place within the tropics that I have visited has such an oppressive climate. I, therefore, determined to make no foolish experiments on this occasion, and not to attempt the descent until I was certain of my pass.

We crawled along the cliff-side for a long way, looking over at every point; but I could see nothing like my old ravine, and soon got fairly puzzled. At last we had followed the mountain ridges almost to the north end of the island, where the plateau of tree-ferns ceases, and where the mountains fall nearly perpendicularly into the sea, and culminate in needle-like peaks, affording no soil for vegetation of any description. So I knew that we had come too far and had passed the entrance to the ravine. We accordingly retraced our steps. We had now exhausted our bottle of water and were suffering from thirst. My old experience had taught me never, if possible, to be far from a stream while wandering over Trinidad. To toil among these arid rocks produces an insatiable thirst, and one's strength fails if one is deprived of water even for a short time. Therefore as we saw below us a ravine that looked like a water-course and which bore some resemblance to the one I was in search of, we decided to explore it. We lowered ourselves down from rock to rock for some way, and soon, to our delight, found a small issue of cool water. But this was not my ravine, for, on descending further, we came to the edge of one of the usual precipices, and we had to clamber up again.

We attempted yet another ravine, which I did not recognise as *the* one, but which might prove to be it nevertheless, for I had to confess that I was quite at sea. This in time led us to a sloping shelf of rock overhanging another precipice. This shelf was extremely slippery, for the stream flowed over it in a thin film and it was covered with a short moss. This, too, exactly corresponds with a description in "Frank Mildmay," that excellent guide to Trinidad, and what is said about the spot in that work may serve as a warning to any—if such there ever be—who may meditate a tour on this island. Two of Mildmay's sailors had been lost while goat-hunting, so he sets forth in search of them. "I was some yards in advance of my companions," he says, "and the dog a little distance from me, near the shelving part of a rock terminating in a precipice. The shelf I had to cross was about six or seven feet wide and ten or twelve long, with a very little inclined plane towards the precipice, so that I thought it perfectly safe. A small rill of water trickled down from the rock above it and, losing itself among the moss and grass, fell over the precipice below, which, indeed, was of a frightful depth. This causeway was to all appearance safe, compared with many which we had passed, and I was just going to step upon it when my dog ran before me, jumped on the fatal pass—his feet slipped from under him —he fell and disappeared over the precipice! I started back— I heard a heavy squelch and a howl; another fainter succeeded, and all was still. I advanced with the utmost caution to the edge of the precipice, where I discovered that the rill of water had nourished a short moss, close and smooth as velvet, and so slippery as not to admit of the lightest footstep; this accounted for the sudden disappearance and, as I concluded, the inevitable death of my dog." Later on, far below, he found "the two dead bodies of our companions and that of my dog, all mangled in a shocking manner; both, it would appear, had attempted to cross the shelf in the same careless way which I was about to do when Providence interposed the dog in my behalf." The adventures of Frank Mildmay and his crew on Trinidad are recorded with such realism and with—as I have before said—such accuracy of local colouring, that I suspect Captain Marryat in this portion of his work is recounting his personal experiences.

So, foiled once again, we reascended the ravine and walked along the edge of the mountains, till we came to a projecting rock that commanded an extensive view over the cliffs. Here we sat down and discussed the problem before us. I assured the doctor that my ravine was certainly close to us somewhere, but that I altogether failed to identify it among the ravines before us, though I carried in my mind's eye a very vivid picture of its appearance.

"Perhaps it has disappeared," suggested the doctor. This seemed scarcely possible, but it might, I acknowledged, have been so changed by landslips as to be unrecognisable.

Being people of logical mind, we reasoned that, if the ravine still existed, we ought now to discover it without any difficulty by a simple process of elimination. There was only a limited number of even possible-looking ways down the precipices. Of these we had now tried two in vain. Again, there were several others which I remembered well to have attempted at the time of my previous visit and to have found impracticable. It followed that we had now to confine our attention to any remaining possible routes, and of these there could be very few.

Indeed, after a careful survey along the edge of the cliffs, we found that there was but one such way left to us, and that looked very ugly. Everywhere else were precipices that could obviously only be descended by a means of progression more rapid than we cared to undertake.

This way seemed as if it might afford a passage to the beach, but it was not a ravine at all. The mountain on which we stood had fallen away, leaving a precipitous step some fifty or sixty feet in height, and from this step there sloped down to a depth, I should say, of quite 1,500 feet a great landslip of broken rocks, the *débris* of the fallen mountain. This landslip appeared to have taken place not long since. It was composed of rocks of all sizes and shapes, almost coal black, piled one on the other at so steep an angle that it was extraordinary how the mass held together and did not topple over. It was indeed in places more like an artificial wall of rough stones on a gigantic scale than a landslip.

The pass I was searching for was utterly unlike this. I remember well that I had found a ravine extending from the mountain top to the beach, which I described in my narrative as "a gloomy gorge with sides formed of black rocks piled on each other in chaotic masses, with a small stream trickling down it." We had experienced little difficulty in ascending or descending it. Before us were now a sufficiency "of black rocks piled on each other in chaotic masses," but no signs of a ravine or stream.

It did not look a tempting route, but we could see nothing else, so decided to try it. The descent was anything but easy and was certainly rather trying to the nerves. To begin with, the descent of the precipitous step I have mentioned was a very creepy business. Having accomplished this without accident we clambered down the giant staircase of black rocks the best way we could, and also with as much speed as was consistent with safety; for the sun was low, the sudden tropical night would soon be on us, and as it would be, of course, impossible to proceed in the dark, we should be compelled to camp out in this very uncomfortable place if we did not hurry on.

We at last reached the foot of the landslip and were on the green down we had seen from above, and which slopes gently to the beach. All our difficulties were over.

These slopes on the windward side of Trinidad are overgrown chiefly with a sturdy species of bean. This plant creeps along the ground, throwing out long tough tendrils, whose mission it evidently is to climb up something for support; but in this they are generally unsuccessful, for nearly all the dead trees have been blown down on this wind-swept corner of the island. A few trees are still standing and these are overgrown with clinging creepers more lucky than the rest. The scene reminded me of countries I had visited where there are ten women to one man and where, consequently, the male is properly appreciated and made much of, while thousands of luckless old maids vegetate hopelessly with no one to cling to. When I imparted this simile to the doctor he implored me not to be sentimental.

The flowers of this bean are pink, and the pods are as large as broad beans. These the doctor at once pronounced to be edible, for, as he explained to me, none of these leguminosæ are poisonous. This was a good thing to know, for they grow so thickly on these shores that we could have collected any quantity we pleased during our stay on Trinidad; and with these, the fish, the turtle, the birds and their eggs, all of which are procurable here without any difficulty, it would be possible for men left on this island to ward off starvation for any length of time.

When I speak of the slopes we were now on as downs, the reader must not conjure up a picture of the grassy downs of the English coast, pleasant under foot and easy to travel on. To drag one's feet over the downs of Trinidad is a very weary business. There are large rocks and deep pits everywhere. One's progress is impeded by the extreme softness of the soil, into which one's feet sink deeply, and this is made still worse by the burrows of the land-crabs, while the roots of the tall grasses and the trailing tendrils of the beans try to trip one up at every step.

Here, to our relief, we found water again. At the foot of the landslip a deep gully opened out which clove the down to the edge of the shore. At the bottom of this a little stream flowed for a short distance, being absorbed by the thirsty soil long before it could reach the sand below.

In order to avoid the entangling vegetation we walked down this gully, and an exceedingly unpleasant place we found it. For here an incredible number of large fluffy white birds, a sort of gannet, were sitting on their nests with their young. They covered the rocks and the branches of the dead trees. They attacked us savagely whenever we came within reach of them, and the whole of the hot narrow gorge stank most offensively of the rotten fish they had strewed about. The different species of birds occupy different portions of this island, and this ravine is the chief haunt of this particular disagreeable tribe.

The whole scene now seemed strangely familiar to me—the ravine, the black rocks, the crowds of brooding white birds—and when at last we came to what appeared to be an old road of piled-up stones crossing the gully I stood still and cried in astonishment: "Why, doctor, this is my ravine after all! I remember this place well!"

Then I looked behind me at the mountain we had descended, and I began to understand how it was that I had been unable to find out my old route. As I have explained, the ravine I had travelled down nine years before extended from the plateau of tree-ferns to the shore. But since then a gigantic landslip had evidently taken place. The mountain-side had fallen away, and millions and millions of tons of rocks had rolled below, entirely filling up the ravine and destroying all traces of it, until far down, where it appeared again on the downs, beyond the limit of the landslip.

This was one among other instances I can mention showing that enormous changes have taken place on this island even in the course of the last nine years. When this terrific fall of rocks occurred, it would have been a wonderful sight to one gazing at it in safety from the sea, and the noise of it must have made itself heard for many leagues around. It has certainly converted what was once a comparatively easy and perfectly safe road from the mountain-tops to the windward shore into an extremely difficult and dangerous one. So much so that the doctor and myself saw at once that it would be useless to establish a depot of stores at the pier, as it would be out of the question to lead the members of the expedition up such a perilous place as this. It was absolutely certain that lives would be lost if this pass were often attempted. No skilful mountaineering would avail against the treacherous rottenness of the precipitous step which surmounts the landslip, and which did not exist of old. There is no certain foothold anywhere upon its face, and we looked forward with no pleasurable anticipation to our enforced return by this way on the morrow.

The birds' eggs lay on every stone in this valley. We tasted some of them, but the flavour bore too much resemblance to the stench of rotten fish around us to be altogether pleasing.

The bank of stones which I had recognised in the ravine was of far too regular formation to be otherwise than the work of men's hands.

Some hundreds of years ago, the Portuguese had a penal settlement on this side of Trinidad, and this, no doubt, was what remained of one of their roads. Some weeks later, I explored the ruins of this settlement, which is a short distance to the north of this gully. I will describe it when I come to that portion of my narrative.

Before we came to the spot where the stream soaks into the earth we filled our bottle with water; then we walked down to the sandy beach, reaching it just before it became too dark to see our way. We were not long in selecting our camp. There was a large rock on the sands above high-water mark, whose hollow side afforded good shelter from wind and rain. In front of this we lit a fire of the wreck wood, of which there was no lack round us, and after a supper of roasted *charki* and biscuit, we proceeded to make ourselves comfortable over our pipes and rum. We were tired, and would have slept very soundly with the sound of the surf on the reefs as our lullaby, had it not been for the land-crabs, which would not let us alone, but pulled our hair or nipped our necks as soon as we began to doze off.

At last their conduct became unbearable, and our patience worn out, so we got up, seized two sticks, and slaughtered some fifty of them. Then we had a little rest, for the others left us alone for a while and devoured their dead brethren, making a merry crackling noise all round us, as they pulled the joints asunder and opened the shells. It was, as the doctor remarked, like the sound of many lobster suppers going on together at Scott's.

At daybreak (Nov. 22) we started for South-west Bay. We had drunk all our water, and so were anxious to reach the bay, explore it, and be back to our stream as quickly as possible. While making this same journey nine years before, I had found no signs of fresh water between this and South Point. The streams that flow from the mountain-tops are absorbed far up by the slopes of *débris* and never reach the shore. Mr. A—— did discover a small, but uncertain, supply near his camp at the head of South-west Bay, but we felt that we could not rely on this, and that the issue in the ravine above us, which we had left on the previous evening, was the only one we could fall back upon with certainty on the whole weather shore of the island.

We walked along the sandy beach, with the mountains towering to the right of us and the ocean swell breaking heavily on the reefs to our left. The beach was covered with wreckage —planks, barrels, spars, timbers of vessels with the corroded iron bolts still sticking in them—a melancholy spectacle; but I was unable to find one particular wreck which I had seen here nine years before—the complete framework of a vessel, partly buried in the sands, into which I had thought it might be worth while for our party now to dig, as some valuables might be lying in her hold. Either the sea had broken up or the sands had completely covered this wreck since my last visit.

We found traces of turtle on the sands, and we saw that the pools of clear water left by the tide were full of fish, while sea-crabs scampered over the rocks in quantities. The beans, too, grew in profusion on the downs above the beach, so there was plenty of food all round us, and, if there had only been fresh water, we could have made ourselves very comfortable here. There were, of course, plenty of land-crabs everywhere, but one would have to be hard driven to eat these ugly brutes.

At last we came to a promontory of rock jutting out into the sea. We climbed up this without difficulty, and descended the other side by a steep slope of soft white sand.

From here we could see before us the Sugarloaf and Noah's Ark. The former mountain, as its name implies, is of conical shape—a stupendous mass, apparently of grey granite, whose summit is about 1,500 feet above the sea, and which on one side is very nearly perpendicular. Noah's Ark (South Point on the Admiralty chart) was so named by myself at the time of my former visit, in consequence of its resemblance both in shape and colour to the favourite toy of my childhood. It is of oblong form, with perpendicular sides and with a top exactly like the roof of a house. It is formed of volcanic rock of a peculiar reddish colour, and is about 800 feet in height. These two strangely-shaped mountains are joined together by an apparently inaccessible ridge composed chiefly of the red detritus from Noah's Ark.

Our destination, South-west Bay, is bounded on its east side by these mountains; it was, therefore, necessary for us now, being south of East Point, to cross the intervening heights.

The only pass I knew was just under the Sugarloaf. This we used generally to speak of as the Sugarloaf Col, so as to distinguish it from another pass which we afterwards discovered. Sugarloaf Col is the gap which divides the Sugarloaf from a jagged peak to the north of it, and which, in its turn, is continued by the steep downs which lie to the back of South-west Bay.

We crossed the sands, and then a small plain covered with a variety of bushes, which brought us to the foot of the Col. This gap is formed of rocks piled on one another, and is not difficult to surmount.

We reached the summit of it and then, looking down on the other side, we beheld, lying at our feet, Treasure Bay at last.

CHAPTER XII

WE EXPLORE THE RAVINE

As we stood on the Col, the steep wall of the Sugarloaf rising to the left of us, the view over South-west Bay was exceedingly fine. The bay is of semi-circular form, with a distance of about a mile and a half from point to point. Broad sands, with green downs behind them, border the central portion; but it is bounded by steep bare mountains on either side: on the east side by Noah's Ark, the Sugarloaf and the peaks beyond; and on the west side by the rugged promontories and islands which divide it from South Bay. In contrast to the savage cliffs that shut them in, the sands and downs in the middle of the bay present a very pleasing and fertile appearance, especially when seen from the sea, conveying the idea that this is a far more agreeable spot to live on than proves to be the case after a closer examination.

From the Col we could look right down on the bay, and, as the water was very clear, we were able to distinguish all the dangers below the surface, as well as those above. It was, no doubt, from here that the pirate captain made his survey.

We saw that an islet, unmarked on any chart, but which I have indicated on my plan, rose in the middle of the bay, while a reef of rocks, apparently coral, extended right around the bay, parallel to the beach and at a short distance from it. Some of these rocks were above the surface of the water, some just below, and others—the most dangerous—further down, so that it was only occasionally that the sea broke upon them. The pirate in his confession had spoken of a channel he had discovered through this reef, situated under the Sugarloaf, at the eastern extremity of the bay. We now saw that it existed there exactly as he had described it—a broad opening in the line of rocks, through which a boat could be pulled, and beached on the sands.

But, still, it was an awkward place, and it would be impossible to land there on such a day as this was, for immense rollers were sweeping up the shore which would have almost certainly dashed any boat to pieces that ventured among them. We were, however, very satisfied with the success of our expedition so far. We had discovered and taken bearings of the channel, and we knew how to pilot a boat through it, when the weather should be favourable. Our next duty was to descend into the bay and identify the place where the treasure was supposed to be hidden.

It was not long before we had discovered what we considered to be the right spot.

The pirate had described a small gully in the middle of this bay, at the foot of which he and his men had erected three cairns, which should serve as landmarks to those who had the clue, and point the way to the treasure.

Mr. P——, and, after him, Mr. A——, had found this gully and the three cairns, just as they had been described. Mr. A——, either for the purpose of putting others off the scent, or in order to discover if anything had been concealed beneath them, blew up these cairns with gunpowder and dug into them, so that now we could only see traces of one of them. He had, however, communicated to me what he understood to be their signification, and how he had been led by them to the first bend in the ravine, at which spot the plunder had been buried under a hollow rock.

We walked up the ravine till we came to a bend, and here, as we had expected, we saw what appeared to be a landslip of red earth, filling up the corner of it, blocking up the mouth of any cave that might exist there, even as Mr. P—— and Mr. A—— had described. And here before us lay a small trench, with a broken earthenware water-jar and the remains of a wheelbarrow lying in it—all that remained to show where Mr. A—— had carried on his not very extensive works.

This, therefore, was the spot we had crossed the Atlantic to find. We stood and looked at it in silence for a while. "What do you think of it?" asked the doctor at last.

It was not an easy question to reply to, for I did not quite know myself what to think of it. I had pictured to myself a very different place. I saw that our work would in one respect be more difficult than I had anticipated, in another respect far more easy. For this landslip was not nearly so extensive as I had understood it to be, and the slopes of the ravine were not of such a character as to render our operations dangerous, or to necessitate any timbering of our shafts or trenches. But, on the other hand, there was a want of definiteness that was disappointing. There were no really sharp bends in the ravine, and there were several landslips. It was impossible to be quite certain of what was meant by "the first bend"; for there were bends of so insignificant a character that they might easily be overlooked; and we had no knowledge of the number of paces from the cairns to the cavern. Therefore, should we fail to find the treasure at the spot where Mr. A—— commenced to dig, it would be necessary for us to clear the landslip off the face of the cliff for some considerable distance.

Having inspected the scene of Mr. A——'s operations, we set out to explore the ravine carefully, and, bearing in mind what we knew of the pirate's original instructions, we endeavoured to reason out whether this or some other neighbouring bend was the most likely spot. The treasure was lying, or had been lying, very close to us somewhere; of that I felt confident at the time, and I have had no reason for altering my opinion since.

First, we went down the ravine again, and when we reached the bottom of it, where it opens out upon the back of the beach, we observed, what had escaped our notice at first, an extensive excavation in the hard soil—which is not so encumbered with boulders here as it is higher up—a cutting so regular in form and with such perpendicular sides that it was difficult to imagine that it had not been the work of men's hands. This was certainly not one of Mr. A——'s trenches; for to have removed such a quantity of earth and stones would have occupied such a party as he had with him for six months at least.

Was it possible that the American, or some other adventurer, had been here before us and carried away the treasure? We could find no marks of tools or other traces of man in or near this trench, so it was impossible to decide whether it was artificial or natural. Some of us afterwards came to the conclusion that it was most probably the latter, for we came across other cuttings, somewhat similar to this, in other portions of the ravine, which had evidently been produced by the action of water.

Next we went up the gully beyond Mr. A——'s trench, in the hopes of finding water, of which we were beginning to feel the want. There was no running stream here, though it was evident from its formation that the ravine was swept by a mighty torrent after heavy rains. The water that drained into it from the overhanging mountain was soaked up by the loose red soil that lay between the boulders.

But at last we came to a little hollow at the foot of a rocky step, where was a tiny pool of tepid and muddy water. However, this was all we required, for we could now afford time to survey the scene of our operations more thoroughly, instead of hurrying back, driven by thirst, to our distant water-course.

Between the hills and the beach, close to the mouth of the ravine, there is a sort of plateau of sand and stones, and it was evidently on this that Mr. A—— had pitched his camp, for here we came across his tent poles, the remains of wheel-barrows, and some empty meat-tins.

We walked down to the eastern beach, where the landing was, opposite the channel between the coral rocks. The sands here sloped steeply into deepish water; it was, apparently, an excellent place for beaching a boat when the state of the weather should allow. Though it was a windless day the ocean swell was high, and it was a grand sight to see the great green rollers sweep majestically up till they were close to the beach, and then curl over and break in showers of sparkling spray. While we stood there admiring the scene, we saw a curious sight. A roller was travelling towards us, rearing its arched neck high up, so that the light of the sun shining through it made it transparent, and in the middle of the clear green mass we saw a long dark body suspended, borne along helplessly. It was a large shark that, venturing too near the beach, had been carried up by the breaker; he floated there a moment, erect on his tail, his fins beating impotently, when the roller broke and he was dashed with a loud thud on the beach; then the recoil of the surf swept him seawards and we saw no more of him.

Having carried out the object of our journey, we filled our bottle with water and set forth on our return march. We recrossed Sugarloaf Col and tramped along the sands. There was no wind and the day was terribly hot. The sands reflected the burning sun into our faces, and we felt as if we were literally roasting. Now and then we lay down, clothes and all, in the salt-water pools, to cool ourselves, and we rolled handkerchiefs round our heads, which we kept constantly wet. As my hat had disappeared over a precipice on the previous day, this was a very necessary precaution against sunstroke, so far as I was concerned.

When we were not far from our previous night's camp, we saw what appeared to be an easier way up the mountains than the one by which we had come down. The precipitous step at the top of the landslip had been difficult enough to descend, and on account of the rottenness of its substance we felt that the ascent might be impossible.

Whether this new way of ours would have led us to the plateau of tree-ferns high above us, I cannot tell; but I doubt it. At any rate, we abandoned it before we had satisfied ourselves as to whether it was a practicable route or not, for a most excellent reason on Trinidad—the want of water. We had exhausted our bottle, and were clambering up difficult declivities on hands and knees, with the fierce sun blazing down upon our backs. As there was no wind, the air that lay on the roasting rocks was so oppressive that we had to rest frequently, and lie on our backs panting for breath.

I was in the worse condition of the two, in consequence of the loss of my hat, for, when the thin handkerchief I had wrapped round my head was dry, it was altogether insufficient for protection, and I ran some risk of being struck down by sunstroke or heat-apoplexy.

Accordingly, as we saw no signs of water above us, and as it was more than likely that this way would lead us to inaccessible

precipices which would drive us back again, we thought it
prudent to retrace our steps before we were quite exhausted,
and make our way to the stream we knew of. We could rest
by it until the sun had dipped below the mountain-tops, and
then resume our climb in the shade.

We descended to the beach, and walked along the sands
until we came to the rock under which we had camped on the
previous night, and then, being opposite to our ravine, we
struck out inland towards it across the down of beans. We
must have turned rather to the right of the track we had
followed on the previous day, for we suddenly came to a
terrace of stones which we had not seen before, and which had
evidently formed part of the Portuguese settlement. We
clambered up this, and then perceived, still further to the right,
the ruins of several huts and walls, built of unhewn stones and
overgrown with the creeping beans. Most of the huts were
built at the edge of a deep steep gully. As soon as we saw this,
the same idea struck both of us: the Portuguese would most
certainly have chosen the vicinity of a stream for their settlement, and in all probability there was running water at the
bottom of that gully.

As it would not take us much out of our way to satisfy our
curiosity, we climbed over the bean-covered rocks until we
came to the edge of the gully, and, looking over, saw, to our
delight and astonishment, not a tiny issue trickling drop by
drop, like most of the streams of these ravines, but a regular
little river of sparkling water, rushing down with a merry
noise over the stones.

We drank our fill, and found the water cool and delicious,
but slightly fishy in flavour, for the large white gannets
thronged the hills above. This is the most considerable stream
on the island, and the only one that reaches the weather shore,
all the others, as I have explained, being sucked up high above
by the slopes of *débris*. This drains an extensive area, and
several ravines meet at the head of the gully, each contributing
its share of water. Among others was one of the ravines we
had attempted to descend on the previous day, and which
had led us to the brink of the precipice. From below we could

see the whole face of that precipice—a fearful wall of black rock, with a thin thread of water falling over it.

We walked down the gully, and found that the stream not only crossed the down, but flowed right across the sands into the sea, the volume of water being too great to allow of its being all swallowed up by the thirsty soil on the way. We should have been more comfortable in our camp on the night before had we known there was a stream so near us, and would have drunk our fill, instead of doling out to each other thimblefuls of water with a grudging hand. It was strange, too, that I had not discovered this river when I was here before. I had then, on descending from the mountains, turned to the right, even as we had done on the previous day, and suffered much from want of water; whereas, had I turned to the left, I should have come upon this generous supply after a few minutes' walk.

This was, indeed, a most valuable discovery for us, for now, should the supply of water fail in South-west Bay, our working party would merely have to cross the Sugarloaf Col, and follow the sands to this river—no very arduous journey.

The heat had been so intense this day that our recent vain climb up the mountain-side had somewhat exhausted us, and we did not feel prepared to accomplish the whole of the long journey to the pier before dark; moreover, the position of the sun showed us that it was long past noon, and we should have had to hurry along without pause, in order to save our daylight.

So we decided to take it easily, and select a camp for the night close to water, on the weather slopes of the mountains. We should have liked to remain where we were, by the river, in the midst of the old Portuguese settlement, but, knowing the difficulties of the homeward journey, we felt that it would be advisable to proceed some way further on our road before camping, and so leave a shorter distance to travel on the morrow.

We accordingly left the river-side and struck across the downs to the foot of the ravine by which we had descended on the previous day. On our way we gathered a quantity of beans for our supper.

We soon found the ravine, and began to ascend it. The foul white birds again attacked us as we climbed from rock to rock, and the ugly crabs waved their pincers at us with menacing gestures. Then we came to the lowest point on the hill-side where water is found. This was at a much greater distance from the beach than it had seemed to be while we were descending on the day before; for the stream disappears in the soil at a spot at least 600 feet above the level of the sea, and to attain it from below involves a pretty stiff climb.

We went still higher up the ravine, until we were close to the place where the stream issues from the ground, a short distance below the foot of the great landslip of black rocks. Here we found an admirable site for our camp. This gully, as I have explained, falls towards the shore at a very steep angle, the rocks, as it were, forming a gigantic flight of steps. We were now on one of these steps, a flat surface, about ten feet across, covered with red sand. The stream fell on to this from the step above, forming a little cascade some twelve feet in height, and, after crossing one side of the flat, fell over another wall of rock on to the step below.

The scene around us was strangely picturesque. Our step was simply a small ledge in this wilderness of broken black rocks; above us and below us were precipices and landslips. It was an excellent situation for an eagle's nest, but not an over-secure spot for a camp of men. Our narrow bed would not do for a restless sleeper: to slip off the edge of it would insure a broken neck. A coarse grass grew here and there between the rocks by the water-side, but there was no other vegetation on the bleak crags, though of course the mysterious dead trees, as everywhere else on this island, were lying thickly all around. The foul birds and the land-crabs were the sole inhabitants of this solitude.

We now proceeded to make ourselves at home for the night. I collected the branches and trunks of the dead trees and built up a goodly pile of firewood, while the doctor prepared our supper. We had no saucepan with us, so the pannikin had to do duty for one. In this the doctor concocted a stew the ingredients of which were *charki*, biscuit, figs, and Trinidad beans.

It turned out to be a far more tasty dish than one would have supposed.

After dinner the saucepan was cleaned out and grog was served out in it—the last of our supply of rum. We had just lit our pipes and were settling ourselves down to a comfortable half hour's smoke and chat before turning in (to whom is a pipe so sweet as to one camping out under the stars after the day's work?) when suddenly the doctor cried out, "Hullo, look at our beds!" I looked, and lo! to my dismay, those luxurious couches were under water.

I must explain that we had pulled up a quantity of grass and strewed it over the sand, so as to make a snug soft sleeping-place for the night. While we were enjoying our dinner, the river, unobserved by us, had risen considerably, and was now flowing over that portion of the step whereon we had made up our beds. There had been no rain to account for this, so I suppose that the sun, blazing down on the rocks, causes a great evaporation of water during the day, and that, consequently, the volume of the streams is greater after sunset.

So we had now to put aside our pipes and grog for a few moments and undertake some necessary engineering operations: we cleared away a channel through the natural dam of grass, stones, and sand at the lower edge of the step, and so gave a free passage to the swollen stream. The flood subsided at once, and our beds were above water again. The doctor, then, acting in his medical capacity, suggested that damp mattresses were unhealthy; so we threw a few handfuls of grass on the top of the sodden mass, and our beds were what we were pleased to call dry again.

We lit a fire of the dead wood and kept it alight all night, so that we could occasionally warm ourselves by it; for a wind had sprung up at sunset, which swept up the ravine from the sea, making us feel uncomfortably chilly, thinly clad as we were and having no blankets to cover us.

We soon found that it would be impossible for us both to sleep at the same time, for the land-crabs had smelt us out and swarmed down upon us from all sides. We kept watch and watch; while one slept the other tended the fire and killed the land-crabs, as they approached, with sticks and stones. The other crabs, as usual, fed on the dead. I have, in the "Cruise of the 'Falcon'," described the peculiarly uncanny way in which a land-crab eats his food. I saw this night, as I kept watch, at least twenty of them at a time devouring the carcases of their slain friends. Each stood quite still, looking me straight in the face with his fixed outstarting eyes, and with an expression absolutely diabolical. He pulled the food to pieces with his two front claws, and then, with deliberate motion, brought the fragments of flesh to his mouth with one claw, and chewed them up with a slow automatic action, but still those horrible eyes never moved, but stared steadily into mine.

As we had no means of judging the time it was difficult to divide the night into watches of even length, so we had to portion it out between us the best way we could.

CHAPTER XIII

A NARROW ESCAPE

WE started early on the following morning, November 23, and reached the summit of the landslip before the sun had heated the black rocks, and the layer of close air immediately over them to that high temperature which we had found so insupportable on the previous day.

We managed to ascend the cliff which hangs over the landslip without accident, but it was anxious work, and we experienced a sense of relief when we found ourselves safe once more on the upper plateau.

From here we took a short cut across the groves of tree-ferns towards the head of the cascade ravine, and came unexpectedly upon a green valley in the middle of the plateau which we had not seen before, and which is, without doubt, the most beautiful place on the island. At the bottom of it a cool stream flowed through thickly-growing ferns and grass. The scenery all round us was of a soft and pleasing character, very strange to us after the dreary barrenness of the mountain slopes beneath this elevated and almost inaccessible garden.

We might have been in some fair vale of Paraguay, instead of on the summit of rugged Trinidad. Here were gently sloping green hills, that shut out all view of the jagged peaks. The vegetation was of a more luxuriant nature than in any other portion of the island; tall grasses, bushes and plants of various kinds, most of them covered with flowers, carpeted the soft red soil, while the tall and beautiful tree-ferns stood in scattered clumps, casting a pleasant shade with their fronds of darker green. Even the dead trees were not so melancholy in appearance as elsewhere on the island; for from their branches —as well as from those of the older bushes and tree-ferns— there hung swaying festoons of a parasitic plant something like the Spanish moss that covers the pines and live-oaks of

Florida, but more beautiful, for this was of a silvery white colour.

Besides those tyrants of Trinidad the birds and land-crabs, mice, flies, ants, earwigs, and big spiders dwelt in this happy valley.

From here we walked to the head of our ravine, where the principal grove of tree-ferns crowns the cliffs, and now we looked down upon the "Alerte," seeming very small from this dizzy height, *"and yon tall anchoring bark, diminished to her cock; her cock, a buoy almost too small for sight."* We observed that the wind was blowing rather freshly from an unusual quarter—north-west—making this a lee shore to our vessel, but there were no signs of bad weather in the sky.

While descending the ravine we were shut in by the walls of rock, so that we were unable to see the yacht; but on reaching a point just above the cascade we again commanded a view over the whole roadstead, and lo! we found, to our dismay, that the "Alerte" was no longer lying at her anchorage, nor was she anywhere in sight.

We stood and stared round the horizon, scarcely believing the evidence of our eyes. Not an hour before we had looked down upon her from the mountain, riding snugly to her anchor, with sails stowed. What possible mischance could have occurred since then?

We proceeded to the pier, on to which we perceived that the sea was breaking much more heavily than when we had landed on it and, from here we were enabled to see further round the coast to the north-west. Then we caught a glimpse of our vessel just before she rounded, and was hidden by, the first promontory. She was about two miles away, with all plain sail set, beating against the wind towards the northern end of the island.

We surmised that those on board had become anxious about our safety, and were sailing round the island, in order, if possible, to discover where we were—a course which they had no right to undertake, seeing that the doctor and myself had not yet been two and a half days away, and were not likely to have lost ourselves. Beside which, I knew that there was no one on board competent to take charge of the vessel on a cruise of this sort. Under these circumstances I was in anything but an amiable temper, more especially as the doctor and myself were now fagged out by our exertions, and had been looking forward to a square meal, and some good red wine with it, on our return on board.

As it appeared that they were bent on sailing round the island, and might not be off the pier again until the following day—for the yacht was evidently progressing very slowly, plunging her nose constantly into the steep head seas—I determined to recall them, if possible. So we hurried back to a slope near the cascade where the grass was growing thickly, and applied a match to it. As I expected, there was soon a great blaze, and a dense volume of smoke arose which must have made itself visible for many miles around. The wind fanned the flames, and the fire crept slowly up the mountainside wherever the dry grass afforded a track for it; the dead trees, too, began to burn fiercely, and we discovered that we had started a somewhat larger conflagration than we had intended, and had set the whole of this side of the island on fire.

However, it produced the desired effect: we saw the yacht sail clear of the point again, on the starboard tack, bear away and run down the coast towards us. And now, at the suggestion, as I afterwards learnt, of Arthur Cotton, who ought to have known better, but who, as having been here before with me, professed to be well acquainted with the pilotage of Trinidad, the anchor was let go, to my horror, quite close to the edge of the breakers. Our vessel was now in very convenient proximity to the end of the pier, it is true, but in a most perilous position: for no sea-room had been allowed her— a very necessary precaution under these cliffs, where the wind is never steady—and I saw that, when the anchor was weighed again, we should run great risk of being carried on to the rocks by the rollers before we could get the yacht under command.

It may be imagined what was my condition of mind when I realised all this, and the doctor was naturally as savage as myself. We stood on the pier and watched the men as they lowered the sails and then launched the whale-boat in order to fetch us off. Powell, Purssell, and two of the paid hands manned the boat. The sea was now so high that they could not approach very near to the shore. The waves were dashing high up the sides of the pier, and, in recoiling, rushed across the end of it in the form of a cascade.

Seeing that we must swim for it, we took off our coats and placed them in a hole at the top of the rocks. I shouted to those in the boat to keep some distance off, and throw a life-buoy with a line attached to it towards the pier, so that we could jump in and be hauled off by it. This was done. Choosing my time I leapt in, held on to the line, the boat was pulled seaward out of reach of the breakers and I clambered on board. Then we returned for the doctor. He stood on the pier, waiting for his opportunity, but one much higher roller than the rest came up and swept him off into the sea. Luckily, he was not dashed against any of the rocks, but managed to swim out clear of the recoil, while we backed towards him and took him on board.

Once safe on the deck of the "Alerte" I listened to an explanation of the extraordinary manœuvres which had been taking place.

It seemed that either the yacht had dragged her anchor or it was supposed that she had dragged her anchor—for the opinions on the matter were at variance—so the anchor was weighed, and, of course, as the chain got short, the yacht, even if she had not done so before, began to drag at a merry pace. Then sail was hoisted. By this time she had drifted very close to the rocks, but, as far as I understand, she was filling and would soon have been in safety again, when, for some reason or other, down went the anchor and she lay rolling about close under the rocky Ness and the dangerous islets that lie off it. Up came the anchor once more, and this time the yacht drove so very near to the rocks that every one on board gave her up as lost, and some were looking out for the safest spot on shore to swim to. A high sea was breaking over the cliffs—one touch and she would have broken up. And now, as by a miracle—for I don't know how it happened, and no one on board seems to have known—the vessel got way on her and forged ahead, so that she became manageable, and was steered out to sea, clear of danger.

That she had been very nearly wrecked there can be no doubt, and that this had been due to very awkward handling was also certain. I was myself much to blame for the serious risk the poor old vessel had incurred. Had I left the doctor in charge on board, in his capacity of mate, while I was exploring the island, he would, no doubt, have extricated the yacht from her difficulty as soon as she began to drag—an easy task. I did not consider that there was any one else among the volunteers capable of undertaking the responsibility of command, but I was under the impression—wrongly it seems—that the five paid hands on board would have had the common sense to give her more chain when they perceived that the wind was freshening. Ted, for instance, was bos'n, and might have taken it upon himself to do this, as was indeed his understood duty when no officers were on board.

For the first and only time during the cruise these men lost their heads, and, having no recognised leader to direct them, each volunteered his own opinion as to what should be done, or as to whether the vessel was dragging at all; but, as far as I can make out, with one man giving one order at one end of the vessel, and another man giving a contradictory order at the other end, nothing at all was done until it was almost too late.

I made up my mind never from this time to leave the vessel, even for a short time, without putting some one definitely in charge, even if he were an incompetent person.

But the danger was not all over yet. The vessel was now tumbling about in the high swell at the edge of the breakers, the wind had dropped, and to have weighed the anchor would have been to have run great risk of being carried on to the rocks by the rollers. So, as she was safe where she was for the time, I saw it was advisable to wait until the conditions should be more favourable, before shifting our anchorage. The doctor and myself enjoyed our square meal to which we had been looking forward, and then I turned in to sleep, giving orders that I should be called at four in the afternoon.

At four the sea had gone down a good deal and there was a moderate breeze, so I decided to move to a safer berth. We hoisted the sails and, while we were getting the anchor up, I took the precaution, seeing what little sea-room we had, of putting the whale-boat in the water, with a long line fastened to the yacht's bows, ready to pull her head round and tow her seawards should she not cant in the right direction.

We got away safely, and the anchor was let go in nineteen fathoms close to where we had brought up on our arrival.

The night was fine, but the surf was still roaring on the beach. The mountains now presented a curious appearance, for our fire had spread up the various arms of the ravine almost to the summit, and there were clusters of lights, as of villages, in all directions, while here and there what appeared to be bonfires were blazing, possibly at spots where several dead trees had fallen together. We began to fear lest the illumination, which must have been visible for leagues out to sea, might attract the attention of passing vessels. A captain would naturally conclude that these fires were the signals of a shipwrecked crew, and therefore go out of his course to render assistance. Luckily this did not happen.

CHAPTER XIV

WE LAND THE STORES IN THE BAY

THE patience of my men was now to be severely tried. Here before them was the mysterious isle, with all its golden possibilities; but for five days the sea was in far too disturbed a condition to permit of a landing; so they were confined to their floating prison, which rolled and pitched at her anchorage all the while, and gazed with vain desire at the forbidden land.

It was now that Ted came up to me, as spokesman for the rest of his shipmates in the forecastle, and said that they were all anxious to go on shore in turn, and do their share of digging with the rest of us. It had been part of the original scheme to keep the paid hands—with the exception, perhaps, of the cook—on board the vessel; but as by this time we knew the ways of the "Alerte," and could handle her with fewer men than when we had started, I decided that an officer and two paid hands would be a sufficient crew while she was lying off the island, and that all the other men could be spared for the work on shore. I therefore acceded to Ted's request.

The men were led to understand that they would be entitled to no share of the proceeds if the treasure were found, though they, of course, knew that, should fortune favour us, a handsome present would be given to them.

The agreement as to the division of the spoil among the gentlemen-adventurers had also to be revised in one respect. It was settled that the shares of those who had abandoned the expedition were to be portioned out among those who remained. By this arrangement each of my companions became nearly twice as rich—in expectations—as when he sailed from England.

Trinidad is supposed to be outside the limit of the south-east trade winds but I think this is doubtful; for, so far as my experience goes, the prevailing winds are from the easterly quarter, and more commonly from the south-east. When the winds are in the west quadrant, and more especially when from the south-west, a heavy sea rises, and landing is rendered altogether impossible. This was our experience for the next few days.

On November 24 there was a high wind from the north-west and a great swell. We were now on a lee shore, and a very dangerous one too; so all was got ready for slipping the anchor and running to the open sea in a moment, should it become necessary to do so. We gave the yacht all her starboard chain —sixty fathoms. We got up the end of the chain, and made it fast to the mainmast in such a way that we could let it go at once. One end of a stout thirty-fathom hawser was attached to the chain just below the hawse-pipe, and to the other end of it we fastened an improvised buoy, made of a breaker and a small bamboo raft. In order to get under way we should now merely have to throw the buoy overboard and cast off the end of the chain from the mast. We could then sail away and leave our moorings behind us.

Then we set to work to bend the storm-trysail, a very handy sail, which could be hoisted much more readily than our heavy mainsail. We reefed the foresail, had a storm-jib ready, and housed our topmast. We were now prepared for anything that might turn up.

We were not idle this day, for after, making all snug, we got the spades, hydraulic jack, and other tools out of the hold, so as to have them in readiness to put in the boat the moment there was a chance of landing.

Our fire on the mountain blazed away all this night and was not entirely extinguished for six days afterwards.

The next day was overcast, and the wind was from the south-west; then it veered to the southward. The sea was higher than on the previous day. The vessel tumbled about a great deal, rolling her scuppers under water, flooding her decks, and running her bowsprit under, all the while. Still, she rode very easily, the great length of heavy chain we had given her acting as a spring. We watched carefully for the first signs of dragging, but the anchor had evidently got a good hold now and she did not budge a foot. In the afternoon the glass fell rapidly and the sky looked very stormy, while the temperature in our saloon fell to 75°, which made us feel quite chilly.

It is probable that this disturbed weather and high sea were the results of a *pampero* raging thousands of miles to the southward of us.

On this day we took our dinghy on deck—a dilapidated little boat—and proceeded to stop her leaks, in a novel, but for the time effectual, manner, with plaster of Paris and tar.

The fish would not be caught while this heavy sea was running, but we secured some sharks and ate their flesh for dinner, to the horror of our black cook, whom I overheard telling his shipmates that he considered it "degrading to eat de meat of de dam shark."

November 26.—Same weather, blowing, raining, rolling, and impatient grumbling of men. Even the two amiable blacks, eager to be at work on shore, fretted a bit at the enforced imprisonment on board. They had always been fond of argument, but now the arguments became stormy, and we could hear them laying down the law to each other in the forecastle, while the English sailors sat round them, smoking in silence and listening with amused wonder. One black was a Roman Catholic, the other a Methodist; their discussions were generally theological, and they exchanged vituperations with a fine theological fury. It was grand to hear Theodosius rail at the Pope and call his comrade a heathen idolater, while George would pour the vials of his wrath on the Methodist heretic. These two poor fellows were the greatest friends, but, of course, each was confident that the other was doomed to perdition. When, in the course of one of these controversies, a theologian found himself caught in a dilemma, he would wax impatient and cry "Oh, chew it!"—an expression I have never heard before—indicating that one has been worsted in argument, but will not allow it, and insists, having had enough of it, on winding up the debate at once.

On the 27th the glass rose, the wind veered to north-east, and the sea moderated; but the surf was still dangerous, and we could see it breaking over a rock sixty feet in height. On this day we sighted two homeward-bound sailing-vessels. During our stay on Trinidad we saw a good many craft, sometimes four or five in a week, all homeward-bounders, for, as I have already explained, it is usual for vessels coming round Cape Horn to make for and sight this island, so as to correct the rate of their chronometers. Few outward-bounders pass it, and it is altogether out of the track of steamers.

On November 28 things looked better, the sea had all gone down. In the morning a few hands pulled off to the pier, where they found the landing perfectly easy, and brought off the coat which the doctor had left on the rock when we had jumped into the sea. My coat could not be found, as it had been washed off by a wave. They also brought off a specimen of a land-crab, which did not seem at all at home on our deck. He was introduced to Master Jacko, our monkey, whose horror at the uncouth apparition was intense. The wise monkey would not get within reach of the crab's nippers, but, having cleverly driven him into a corner, tried to push his ugly visitor through a scupper into the sea with a bit of firewood.

I must now apologise to Jacko for not having before this introduced him to my readers. He was a delightful little creature that we had purchased on the Praya at Bahia. He was very affectionate, and was free from malice, though, of course, full of mischief. He had a red blanket of his own, which he would carry about with him wherever he went, and, should a few drops of rain fall or spray come on board, he would deftly roll it about him in the fashion of a cloak, with his funny little head just peeping out of the hood. He was very fond of tea, and while we were at sea he took his 4 A.M. cup with the others. As soon as the cook began to lift the boiler of tea from the stove Jacko would give a whistle of delight, clamber up the pantry wall, unhook a pannikin, and walk up with it to be filled, "all de same as a little ole man," as the cook used to say. It was amusing to see him test the temperature of the tea with his fingers before drinking it. He was a marvellously intelligent and jolly little creature, and is now dwelling happily in a little house on a cocoanut tree in a plantation near Port-of-Spain. He prefers a West Indian life of warmth and unlimited bananas to an existence in a damp ship on salt junk and biscuit.

At noon, as the sea was still smooth, we made our first attempt at landing in Treasure Bay. We put the whale-boat in the water, and loaded her with about a ton of stores, consisting of tinned provisions of various sorts, biscuit, salt beef, the picks, spades, crowbars, wheelbarrows, hydraulic jack, and other tools. We also took in tow a raft constructed of the long bamboos we had brought from Bahia. These we knew would be useful for several purposes.

I steered the boat, while the doctor, Powell, Purssell, and two paid hands, took the oars. Having the wind behind us we were not long in crossing the two miles of smoothly heaving sea that lay between us and South-west Bay. We rounded the point into the bay, and, leaving on our port hand the islet in the middle, we made for the channel which the doctor and myself had surveyed from the mountains. When we came near we found that there were three parallel lines of breakers to be traversed, and, consequently, there was a treble chance of swamping. The surf was much more formidable than we had expected to find it, considering how smooth the sea was outside the bay. The wind was blowing in strong gusts right off shore, over the depression in the mountains at the back of the bay. It drove off the tops of the oncoming waves into great veils of spray, curling over in a contrary direction to the curl of the swell, and bright with shifting rainbows as the sun's rays fell upon it. The bay presented a most beautiful appearance from the boat, and those who had not seen the pirates' haunt before uttered exclamations of admiration and wonder. Between the gloomy black mountains on the left and the unearthly-looking dark red walls of Noah's Ark on the right was a scene in which, flooded with tropical sunlight, earth and ocean vied with each other in vividness of colouring. Directly in front were the great rollers of transparent green, their snowy crests flashing with rainbows; beyond, dazzling golden sand; above, domes of brilliant emerald cleaving the cloudless sky.

But this was no time to dwell on the beautiful; we had other matters to consider. The grand rollers with their breaking tops had no charms for us, for we had to get through them—a risky undertaking with a deeply-laden boat.

We discovered afterwards that it is almost impossible to judge from the height of the swell near our anchorage, or from the surf on the pier, whether landing in South-west Bay is likely to be easy or the reverse. The surf on this sandy beach is governed by a different system of laws to that which prevails on other portions of the coast of Trinidad. Here, curiously enough, there is more surf when the wind is blowing off shore than when it is blowing on. The north-east wind, sweeping in violent gusts down the slopes that back the bay, offers a resistance to the swell rolling in, and piles it into steep walls of water, breaking dangerously. The south-east wind raises a higher swell outside, but, blowing right into this bay, drives the sea down, and the landing becomes comparatively easy. At the anchorage opposite the cascade the contrary is the rule: with a north-east wind blowing off shore the sea is smooth, with a south-east wind the surf increases; but, as I have already stated, it is always smoother there than in South-west Bay.

The men rested on their oars, and we watched the surf from a safe distance, to discover if there were any chance of picking a favourable opportunity for landing. It would be a disappointing matter if we had to pull our boatload of stores back to the yacht against the wind; so, after a little hesitation, I decided to risk the landing. One must run some risks on such a place as Trinidad, and we might as well commence at once. All in the boat were delighted at the decision.

Everyone knows how the ocean swell proceeds in regular rhythm, and how one sees at intervals three greater waves than usual come up, one after the other, to be succeeded by a comparative calm. We took the boat just outside the outer breakers and awaited one of these smoothes. Soon three great waves passed under us, and broke beyond us with terrific force. Now was our time, and we made a dash for it. The long ash oars bent as the men, putting their backs into their work, drove the boat through the sea. Pull away! Pull away! The first row of breakers is passed; then we are safely borne on the top of the second, looking down upon the beach as from a hill. It passes us and breaks. All safe so far. We are close to the beach. Then, behind us, we see a wall of water suddenly rise, curling over. We should simply be rolled over it we tried to back the boat against it, so the men strain at their oars to reach the shore before it. The boat is just touching the sand, the order is given: "All hands overboard and haul her up," when the sea pours over our heads, filling the boat. The men leap or are washed overboard. One catches hold of the long painter we had provided in view of such an emergency and contrives to reach the shore; then, planting his heels in the sand, he holds on with all his strength, to prevent the boat being swept off into deep water by the receding wave. At first the other hands are out of their depth, but, as the roller recoils, they feel bottom; then, two of us holding on to one side of the boat and two on the other, while the remaining man scrambles on shore to assist the man with the painter, we haul the boat up till she grounds; then we all stand by till the next roller comes on to help us up a bit further. Here it comes! right over our heads, and we are afloat once more. But the two men on shore haul away with all their might, as do the others when they touch bottom, and when the wave recoils it has left us fifty feet higher up the bank, and out of reach of any heavy body of water.

It was lucky for us that ours was a lifeboat with a water-tight compartment at either end or we should not have got out of this scrape so well. The boat did not capsize when she filled, neither did she broach to, her head was always direct for the shore. The tide was coming in fast, so we lost no time in getting her safely drawn up. While some hands took out the stores and tools, others baled her out, and, by placing bamboo rollers under her, we dragged her up the steep incline of sand until she was quite out of reach of the sea. We found that we had not lost or damaged any of our stores, so had good reason to congratulate ourselves on our success.

A tot of rum was served to all hands after their exertions,

and then we carried all our property up to the spot we had selected for our camp—a plateau of sand and earth opposite the mouth of the ravine.

Then, as all were, of course, anxious to see the supposed hiding-place of the treasure, the doctor and myself took them to it. On ascending the gully somewhat higher than we had gone on our previous visit we discovered two or three small pools of inferior water. But the supply was insufficient, even after the recent heavy rains; so it was evident that, unless we found some other source, our condensing apparatus would not have been brought in vain. There was, fortunately, an abundance of fuel in the neighbourhood, for the dead trees were strewed over all the hill-side.

We had not brought off any of the tents, but, with a good fire and plenty to eat, drink, and smoke, there would be little hardship in sleeping out; and the doctor and Powell volunteered to stay on shore, while I went back to the yacht. It was my intention to return, if possible, on the following day, with the tents and other stores, and to then leave a working-party on the island. We might, of course, on the other hand, be prevented by a heavy sea from landing again for a week or more; so we bade our comrades an affectionate farewell, and enjoined them not to be lazy, but to dig away until they saw us again—a quite unnecessary suggestion, for they were very keen to begin work.

Taking with me Purssell and the paid hands, we hauled the boat down to the beach; we dragged her into the water quickly, just as one big roller was recoiling, jumped in and pulled hard out to sea. We shipped a little water at the second line of breakers, and were then in safety.

We soon found, as we pulled back to the yacht, that our boat had sprung a leak, for the water was pouring in fast through her bottom, so that we had to stop and bale occasionally. She was an excellent sea-boat, but lightly built, and her bump on the sands had done her no good.

CHAPTER XV

OUR CAMP

WE hoisted our leaky lifeboat into the davits when we got on board, intending to repair her on the following morning.

During the night fierce gusts blew down the ravine from the north-east, and black masses of cloud were constantly sweeping across the mountains. The wind howled as it does in a wintry gale on the North Sea, and, to all appearance, a heavy storm was raging. Still, it was quite smooth at our anchorage under the lee of the island, and we noticed that seawards the sky looked fine enough, and the clouds were travelling at no great pace. The storm, in fact, was entirely local, and was limited to the islet and its immediate neighbourhood. We afterwards became quite accustomed to these harmless gales, which had a habit of springing up at sunset.

Trinidad, in consequence of the loftiness of its mountains, can boast of a climate of its own. It is subject to miniature cyclones, whose influence does not extend a mile from the shore, and which, therefore, cannot raise a heavy sea. We were sometimes riding with straining chain to a wind of hurricane force, when we could see a vessel a league or so from the land making no progress, her canvas shaking in the calm; and, however fine it might be outside, the clouds would collect upon the peaks in ominous torn masses, that whirled along as if impelled by a terrific blast, and which looked very alarming until we came to understand the innocence of the phenomenon. We also found that the landing was often the most perilous on clear, windless days, when no clouds crowned the mountains.

These storms were, however, a nuisance to us; for the squalls would strike the yacht with great force, so that she strained at her chain and was likely to drag; consequently the officer in charge was unable to enjoy an undisturbed night's rest, but was in a state of constant anxiety for the vessel, and was often brought on deck by the turmoil to satisfy himself that all was going well.

The next day, November 29, was fine, the wind being still from the north-east. There was even less swell than on the previous day, so we saw that no time must be lost in landing more stores. A neglected opportunity on Trinidad might mean a month's delay.

We examined the boat, and found that she had started a plank, but that the damage was slight and could be easily repaired. A few copper nails, some cotton thrust between the seams with a knife, and a little marine glue, made her right again; and, after breakfast, she put off to Treasure Bay with a miscellaneous cargo, the tents, a barrel of flour, wire-fencing, the blankets and baggage for the shore-party, &c.; but we did not venture to put nearly so heavy a weight into her as on the previous day.

The surf in the bay was no longer dangerous, and, though water was shipped, all was landed without accident. At mid-day the boat returned to the yacht, was reloaded, and another successful disembarkation was effected. This put us in very good spirits. We had succeeded in overcoming the difficulties that had caused previous expeditions to fail, and had now got on shore all that was absolutely necessary for carrying on the digging for some time to come. The doctor, Purssell, Powell, and Ted Milner were left on shore for the night, and the boat returned to the yacht.

The next day, November 30, was the first on which we divided ourselves definitely into two parties, the working-gang on shore and a crew of three to take charge of the yacht. I had talked our plans over on the previous day with my sole officer, our medico-mate, and we came to the conclusion that it would be advisable for me to stay on board for the first fortnight, at least; for we did not know as yet whether it would be safe to remain at anchor for any length of time, or what steps might become necessary in order to ensure the safety of the vessel; and, until such knowledge had been gained by experience of the conditions of the place, it was right that I should undertake the responsibility of looking after the yacht.

So, on this morning, I went on shore for the last time, before settling down to my fortnight's watch. We took another cargo of stores in the boat, and landed without difficulty. This long spell of smooth sea was a most fortunate occurrence for us.

On landing I found that the shore-party had been hard at work. They had arranged the camp—and very snug it looked. Two ridge tents had been placed side by side, to be occupied by the gentlemen volunteers, two in each; while a short way off was a larger tent, constructed of our racing spinnaker and the quarter-deck awning supported by bamboos. This was our dining-room and kitchen, and also served as sleeping quarters for the paid hands. At one end of it was an elegant dining-table—planks from the deck of some old wreck, supported by one of Mr. A——'s wheelbarrows which had been found in the ravine. A few campstools and barrels served as chairs, and the arrangements generally were almost luxurious.

Many improvements were made to the camp during our stay in Trinidad, and at last it became a comfortable little village. A conspicuous object near the tents was the condensing apparatus. Later on, the cooking was all done out of doors, a neat oven having been constructed of stones and plaster of Paris. The plaster of Paris had formed part of the taxidermist's stores, but, little used for its original purpose, it was found to be of much service in the way of cement.

A list of all that we landed on the shore of South-west Bay would be a long one. There was, at the very least, eight tons weight in all. I need not say that the cook was well provided with culinary apparatus, and that such articles as paraffin lamps for the tents, a library of books, fishing lines and hooks, and carpenter's tools had not been forgotten—our camp, in short, was fully furnished with everything that could be required.

The doctor and myself discussed the scheme of work on shore, and, when all was settled, we launched the boat again and pulled off to the yacht. It was decided that the shore-party should keep the whale-boat—in the first place, because the crew on board would be insufficient to man her, and, secondly, because it was only right and prudent to leave a boat on the island in case of any accident happening to the yacht. It would be easy for the working-party to pull off, if necessary, and intercept a passing vessel. The dilapidated dinghy was left on board for our use.

The hands who had come off in the boat dined on board, and then the doctor, taking with him those who were going to stay on shore, pulled back to the bay, to commence his duties as Governor of Trinidad, leaving me with my two hands, Wright and the coloured man Spanner. And a very good governor the doctor proved too, as I discovered when I next went on shore and saw the work that had been got through. He kept up a discipline quite strict enough for all practical purposes. He did more work than any one else himself, being physically the strongest man of us all, and he superintended all the operations with great skill and judgment. The control could not have been left in better hands, and he was well backed up by his comrades. There was hard work done on that island, considerable hardships were undergone, there was often dangerous landing and beaching of boats, and all was carried on under a vertical sun on one of the hottest and most depressing spots on earth. Great credit is due to the doctor and the others who worked so hard and with such pluck and cheerful zeal, and the ungenerous remarks of the one dis-contented volunteer we had left—a man who did not do his share of work either at sea or on shore, but who did far more than his share of criticism and fault-finding—can only reflect upon himself. As he had favoured the world with his sneers through the medium of the papers, I feel bound to say this much.

The doctor remained and worked hard on the island during the whole time that our operations were being carried on, as did Powell and Purssell, and they, with the paid hands, who relieved each other at intervals, practically did all the digging. I was on shore for one fortnight only, as will appear in the course of this narrative. I had, consequently, but a very small share of the hard work and of roughing it, for the life on board ship was incomparably more comfortable and easy than the life on shore. Our critical volunteer also only passed about two weeks, of not arduous work, on the island; for the rest of the time he was on the yacht.

This night we had another local storm, but by now we were getting accustomed to this.

Shortly after dawn on the following morning, Sunday, December 1, I saw, to my surprise, the whale-boat rounding the point. She came alongside, and the doctor, who was in charge of her, boarded us. Seeing that there was very little surf in South-west Bay, he had rightly taken the opportunity of putting off for another cargo of stores. Among other articles, he carried away some large cocoanut mats we had purchased at Bahia, and which, when laid on the sandy floor of the tents, would make things more comfortable. He also took off the heavy boiler and receiving-tank of the condensing apparatus, which could only be landed on a favourable day such as this was. Having loaded the boat, he left us again.

We had now taken so much weight out of the yacht that she was high out of the water, and might possibly prove somewhat cranky under canvas. So, after dinner, I took the two men off with me in the dinghy, for the purpose of fetching some heavy stones from the beach, to put in our hold in the place of all the tools we had taken out. First we pulled to the pier, where we landed without the slightest difficulty. Wright, while wandering about the beach, came across the last object one would expect to find on a desert island—a rather smart lady's straw-hat, so far as my judgment goes, of modern fashion. It had, probably, been blown off some fair head on a passenger steamer. The gallant gentlemen-adventurers, when they heard of this discovery, proposed that it should be stuck on a pole in the middle of the camp, to remind them of home and beauty.

Finding that there were no suitable stones near this beach, we got in the boat again and rowed to West Bay, to see if we should have better luck there. Three islets—as indicated in the plan of Trinidad—lie off the east side of the Ness. We found that the narrow deep-water channel between these and the cape could be taken with safety on a fine day like this. As a

rule, this channel is impracticable, for the ocean swell pene-
trating it produces a great commotion, the sea being dashed
with violence from the cliffs on one side to those on the other,
so that the entire channel presents the appearance of a boiling
cauldron; and, even on this quiet day, we had to keep the
boat carefully in the middle, for the waves leapt high up the
rocky walls with a loud noise, which was repeated in manifold
echoes by the crags above. When we were in the passage
between the third islet and the shore the scene before us was
most impressive. The black cliffs rose perpendicularly on
either side of us, about thirty feet apart, casting a profound
shade on the heaving water, so that it looked like ink beneath
us; and between these cliffs, as through a dark tunnel, we saw
the sunlit waters and shores of West Bay. The mountains that
lay to the back of it were barren and of bold outline, great
pinnacles of rock dominating huge landslips that slope to the
shingle-beach. We could distinguish the familiar forms of the
Sugarloaf and Noah's Ark towering over the depressions of
the hills.

At the further end of the bay we found a suitable place for
getting stones. Here a rocky shelf formed a sort of jetty.
George leapt on shore and brought down the stones, while
Wright, sitting in the stern, took them from him, and placed
them at the bottom of the boat, while I backed in towards the
jetty and pulled out again between the waves; for there was
sufficient sea to do damage if proper caution was not observed.
Having taken on board about half a ton of large heavy stones,
we returned to the yacht and stowed them under the cabin-
floor.

On the following morning, December 2, the doctor came
off again in the lifeboat, and carried off another moderate
load of stores. He reported that on the previous day, being
Sunday, he had given all hands a holiday on his return to the
shore, and that they had passed the day in exploring the
neighbourhood of Treasure Bay. They came across some more
tent poles and picks left by Mr. A——'s party. They also
made one very curious discovery—a quantity of broken
pottery, lying in a little rocky ravine at a considerable height

above the shore. All this was of Oriental manufacture. Some was of unglazed earthenware, some of glazed china—the remains of what appeared to have been water-jars and punch-bowls. There were also some broken case-bottles of glass, oxidised and brittle from long exposure. The bowls proved to be of Blue Dragon china, about a hundred years old, and, therefore, of some value to the connoisseur.

Pottery of this description had certainly not formed part of the equipment of Mr. A——'s, or of any other of the treasure-hunting expeditions. Could these be relics of the pirate's booty—articles they had thrown away as being of no value to them when they buried the rest of the treasure? It was, certainly, difficult to account for the presence of old blue china on a barren hill-side of Trinidad. It has been suggested by an old sea-captain that an East-Indiaman may have been wrecked here many years ago, and that her crew had contrived to reach the shore with provisions and other property, for bowls of the same description as those of which these fragments had formed part were commonly used by the Malay sailors to eat their curry in.

The doctor soon left me, and hurried back with his boat's crew to the camp, for the sea was rising, the glass had been falling for twenty-four hours, and the sky had a stormy appearance, not only over the mountains, but on the sea-horizon as well.

These signs of foul weather did not deceive us, for it now blew hard from the south-east for several days, and the sea was so rough that we were unable to launch the dinghy, while, on the other hand, it was impossible to put out from the bay in the whale-boat. All communication was, therefore, cut off between the yacht and the shore for six days, and we could not even see each other during this time, as two capes stretched out between us.

It was fortunate that we had landed such an ample supply of stores while the weather was fine.

We had rather an uncomfortable time of it on board for the next few days. For a good part of the time the wind was blowing with the force of a gale, and it howled and whistled

among the crags in a dreadful fashion, while the surf thundered
at the base of the cliffs. The wind being south-east was parallel
to this portion of the coast; so we were scarcely, if at all, protected by the island. A great swell rolled up, travelling in the
same direction as the wind. But as violent squalls occasionally
rushed down the ravines at right angles to the true wind, we
were blown round by them, so that we were riding broadside
on to the sea, rolling scuppers under in the trough of it, pitching the whole bowsprit in at one moment and thumping our
counter on to the water the next.

Things looked so bad on December 4 that I was thinking of
slipping the anchor and putting to sea, but, as the vessel did
not appear to be straining herself, I held on. Our dinghy was
dipping into the sea as we rolled, so we took it from the davits
and secured it on deck.

We had now ample leisure to study the meteorology of
Trinidad. The rains were heavy during this stormy period and
the cascade swelled visibly. I do not think this island is subject
to drought; for, notwithstanding that this—the summer—was
the dry season here, scarcely a day passed without a shower
during our long stay. In the winter season this is, to judge
from the logs of passing vessels, a very rainy spot. The glass
never fell below thirty inches while we were here, and generally
stood at about thirty and two-tenths. The temperature in the
shade on board averaged about eighty. In the tents on shore
it was far hotter. The sunsets are often very fine on Trinidad,
of wild and stormy appearance and full of vivid colouring;
these indicate fine weather. The boisterous south-west winds,
extensions of River Plate *pamperos*, are heralded by clear blue
skies.

We three now imprisoned on the yacht occupied our time
in tidying her up, and making all necessary repairs in the sails
and gear generally. We occasionally knocked down some
birds as they flew over us. Some would coolly perch on our
davits and stare at us very rudely, to the great indignation of
Jacko, who swore at them in his own language. It was curious
to watch the birds fly far out to sea each morning for their
day's fishing, the air full of their shrill and melancholy cries,

and return again in the evening. It was invariably while starting at daybreak that they called on the yacht. While going home in the evening they had their business to attend to. It was then that they carried food to their young—fluffy balls of insatiable appetite, which, I am afraid, had sometimes to go to bed supperless; for the anxious mothers are often robbed of their hard-earned fish by the cruel pirates who are perpetually hovering round this island.

These pirates are the frigate or man-of-war birds. They do not fish themselves, but attack the honest fishers in mid-air, and compel them to surrender what they have caught. The frigate-bird is of the orthodox piratical colour—black—but has a vermilion beak and a few white patches on its throat. It has a forked tail, and wings of extraordinary length in proportion to its body, their spread sometimes attaining, it is said, as much as fifteen feet.

There are other pirates here as well, of a meaner description, who, being able to fish for themselves, have no excuse for their crimes; whereas the frigate-bird is unable to skim the sea after fish. Should he touch the water he cannot make use of his unwieldy wings, and flounders helplessly about until he becomes the prey of sharks.

But these other robbers have taken to dishonest ways from sheer laziness and lack of principle. Their favourite method is to seize a smaller fisher by the throat, and hold him under water until he is half drowned and has to disgorge his fish. Sometimes two or three plucky little birds will assist a neighbour in resisting the big bully, and often drive him off discomfited. We witnessed several most exciting combats of this description.

We skinned the birds we killed, and I have brought these specimens home with me. Of fish we now caught plenty. We salted and sun-dried some, but these were not a great success, and had a rank flavour in consequence of their oily nature.

CHAPTER XVI

DISCOVERIES IN SOUTH-WEST BAY

AT last, on December 7, communication between the yacht and the shore was resumed; for the wind and sea had greatly moderated, and the doctor was enabled to come off to us at midday, with four volunteers and paid hands. They had been labouring hard with pick and shovel, and looked like it, too. Digging into the volcanic soil of Trinidad soon takes all superfluous flesh off. Indeed, led on by the energetic doctor, they had worked harder, perhaps, than white men should in such a climate, and had a stale, overstrained appearance, while they admitted that they felt somewhat slack.

They brought us off a quantity of turtle-eggs. The female turtle frequent South-west Bay in large numbers, for the purpose of depositing their eggs in the sand. But up till now, they had failed to catch any of the turtle. The eggs are excellent, and can be used for every purpose for which fowl's eggs are employed. Here is a receipt for making egg-nog which I have tried myself and can recommend:—Two turtle eggs, a tea-spoonful of tinned milk, some water, sugar, and a small glass of rum.

The shore-party had obtained an abundance of fish; they used to catch them not only with hook and line, but with an extemporised seine net, which they dragged with great success through the pools left by the receding tide. This seine was simply a long piece of the wire-netting which we had brought with us to serve as land-crab-proof fencing round the camp. It seems that this netting did not fulfil its original purpose very satisfactorily, as the crabs could burrow under it.

The land-crabs, however, did not molest the shore-party to any extent, and it was only now and then that a man found one of these unpleasant creatures in his bed. It was the custom for the men to sally forth every evening, just before dark, and kill, with sticks, every land-crab they could find in the immedi-

146

ate neighbourhood of the camp, each man slaying his sixty or seventy. This afforded an abundance of food for the others during the night, so that they had no need to stray into the tents. The crabs, I was informed, were excellent scavengers, and consumed all the cook's refuse.

The doctor and his companions had no lack of news to impart. I was anxious, of course, in the first place, to learn how the work had progressed. I was told that some hundreds of tons of earth had been already removed, and that a broad trench was being dug, along the face of the cliff, through the landslip in the first bend of the ravine, but that, so far, no indications of the treasure had been come across. The chief difficulty consisted in the presence of a great many stones of all sizes that were mixed up with the fallen soil, some of them being of several tons weight. In digging the trench, an inclined plane was left at either end, up which the barrows of earth could be wheeled; and when one of the big stones was found, the earth was, in the first place, cleared from round it, and then it was dragged from the bottom of the trench up one of these inclined planes by means of powerful tackle, assisted by the hydraulic jack. When they had got it by these means to the top of the trench, they could easily roll it down the ravine.

The doctor explained to me all the routine that he had laid down for observance on shore, and the different details of the work. Sunday was always a holiday, and was occupied, as a rule, in wandering about and exploring; but it was sometimes too terribly hot for this.

I was informed that a crowbar and several other fresh relics of Mr. A——'s expedition had been discovered, and that a wooden box had been found carefully hidden away at the further end of the bay, which contained a chess-board, a quantity of shot cartridges, and several London and New-castle newspapers, dated October 1875. Mr. A——'s expedition took place in 1885, Mr. P——'s—the first expedition—in 1880; so the papers gave us no clue as to who had brought them here. The shore-party had amused themselves by reading these ancient journals. In them they found accounts of the

Wainwright trial and of the collision between the "Mistletoe" and the "Alberta." It was strange to read, on Trinidad, the old theatrical advertisements in the *Standard*, with Charles Matthews acting at the Gaiety and Miss Marie Wilton at some other house. There was an excellent notice of the latter charming actress in one of these papers.

I was told that there had not been so much surf in Southwest Bay as might have been expected with so strong a wind; but, as I have explained, the south-east is the wind that raises the least surf on this sandy beach, though it blows right on to it.

The doctor told me that they had experienced, on every occasion they had landed, a strong current sweeping along the shore of the bay in an easterly direction, so that, no sooner did the bow of the boat touch the sand, then her stern was driven round by the current to the left, and, unless proper precautions were taken, she would get broadside on to the next sea and be rolled over.

On being asked whether they had had much rain in the bay, they replied that the showers had been as heavy as those tropical downpours we had experienced in the doldrums. They said that the Sugarloaf presented a magnificent appearance after one of these showers, for then a cascade 700 feet in height would pour down its almost perpendicular sides. They had been enabled to fill their tanks and breakers with rain-water, and had only used the condensing apparatus on one or two occasions, and then more by way of experiment, to see how it worked, than from necessity. It acted perfectly, and with it five gallons of fresh water were distilled from sea-water in a very short time.

The fortunate discovery had also been made of two small issues of water among the cliffs at the east end of the bay. The supply was sufficient, and though the carrying of the water in breakers from here to the camp over the rough ground entailed heavy labour, it was easier to fetch it in this way than to collect the large quantity of firewood necessary for condensing an equal amount of water.

The doctor reported Arthur Cotton as being ill, and unfit for further digging for the present; so he was left on board with me, while George went on shore to take his place. The doctor promised to come off for me on the following morning, so that I could pay a short visit to the shore and inspect the works—provided, of course, the surf permitted. Then we bade each other farewell, and the working-party returned to the bay.

The boat did not come off to me on the following day, as the surf was dangerous in South-west Bay; and I held no communication with the shore-party for another week. During this time the wind was from the south-east; but though it rushed down the ravine with the usual violent squalls, it was moderate outside, and we had no more of the heavy sea which had been running throughout the previous week. It would have been possible for me to have landed at the pier on nearly any day, but there was still a sufficient surf to prevent our carrying off any more stones from the shore.

We were anchored on a sandy bottom, but we could feel, by the grumbling of our chain as the yacht swung, that there were many rocks under us as well. These caused us a good deal of annoyance; for on several occasions, when the vessel was lying right over her anchor, the slack of the chain would take a turn round a rock and give us a short nip; so that when a swell passed under us, the vessel could not rise to it, but was held down by the tautened chain, which dragged her bows under, producing a great strain. The rocks must have been of brittle coral formation, for, after giving two or three violent jerks as the sea lifted her, the vessel would suddenly shake herself free with a wrench, evidently by the breaking away of the obstruction. At last all the projecting portions of the coral rock in our immediate neighbourhood must have been torn off, the chain having swept a clear space for itself all round, for after a time we were no longer caught in this way. These great strains loosened our starboard hawse-pipe badly, so that we had to slip our chain and pass it through the other hawse-pipe.

On December 9, it being a very fine day, I made an expedition in the dinghy toward the north end of the island. We found no good landing-place in that direction, for a coral ledge extends along the whole coast, causing broken water, and there are dangerous rocks in the midst of the breakers. We pulled into several little bays, each hemmed in by inaccessible barren mountains, so crowded with birds that, from the sea, the black crags looked quite white with them. We pulled inside Bird Island and inspected the Ninepin from close to. This huge cylinder of rock, 900 feet in height, is described by old navigators as having been crowned with large trees. It is now completely bare of vegetation, as it also was when I first saw it in 1881. I observed that, since my last visit, a huge mass had fallen off the top of it, which now lay by its side in shattered fragments. We caught a quantity of fish in these bays, one a fine fellow weighing thirty pounds; and we saw several large turtle floating on the water, but they sank as soon as we got near them.

The uneventful days passed by and I grew stout on laziness, salt beef, and duff. At last, on December 14, we pulled off in the dinghy to South-west Bay, to see how the shore-party was getting on. We took with us a signal code book and the flags, so as to converse with our diggers in case we could not effect a landing—a feat not to be attempted with our rotten little dinghy except under the most exceptional circumstances. The shore-party was, of course, also provided with a code book and set of flags.

As I required some more specimens of birds, I took with me, not a gun with which to shoot them, but simply a ramrod, the end of which I had loaded with a piece of lead. With this, as I sat in the boat, I found no difficulty in knocking down the inquisitive birds as they flew just over our heads, and I thus procured several good specimens.

When we had pulled round the point and were in South-west Bay we saw the white tents of the camp in front of us, and we could plainly distinguish, in the ravine behind, the great trench which the men had dug at the side of the cliff. We found little surf in the bay, but I would not risk a landing; for it would not require much bumping to knock our dinghy's ancient bottom off; so we remained outside the breakers and signalled: "Any news?"

There was no reply with the flags, but some of the men

walked down to the rocks under the Sugarloaf, so that we could come near enough to them to hail. A very disreputable lot our friends looked, too: as unkempt and rough as the original pirates might have been. The costume of each consisted merely of shirt, trousers, and belt, some sort of an apology for a hat crowning all. They were all more or less ragged, and were stained from head to foot with the soil in which they had been digging, so that they presented a uniform dirty, brownish yellow appearance, and, from a passing vessel, might easily have been taken for Brazilian convicts.

They shouted what news they had to tell. They reported that they were progressing well with the digging, and that they had caught a number of turtle. They promised to come off to the yacht the next morning, surf permitting. I made some sketches of Treasure Bay and West Bay as seen from the sea, and then returned to the vessel, to skin my birds.

The whale-boat was alongside on the following morning, December 15, and the doctor, Powell, Pollock, and two paid hands, boarded us. They had brought off some fresh and salted turtle and a quantity of turtle eggs.

The yacht had now been lying off Trinidad for twenty-five days, and the shore-party had been hard at work for seventeen days; so I thought it was quite time for me to join the camp, and do my share of the work. I could see that the energetic doctor was anything but anxious to change the hard labour on shore for the lazy life on board ship, and though, as mate, he would have been the proper person to take charge of the vessel during my absence on land, still we considered it advisable to arrange matters differently.

The doctor, as I have said, was a most useful man on shore, and, as we were anxious to complete our operations as quickly as possible and leave the island before the stormy season should set in, it seemed a pity to waste so much energy and muscle as his in an idle life on board the yacht. Having remained at anchor for so long, and knowing that our anchor had now got such a firm hold that there was but little chance of its dragging, and having, moreover, discovered by experience that it was possible to ride where we were even in bad weather,

I had acquired a considerable confidence in the safety of the vessel, and I believe that she could have remained off the cascade for six months without suffering damage. I, therefore, now came to the conclusion that it would not be very imprudent to leave a somewhat incompetent person in charge, as the chances were that he would have nothing to do. Pollock, who had complained of slackness for some time, was the one from whom the least amount of work could be extracted on shore, and was, therefore, the one who could be the most easily spared. I, consequently, decided to leave him on board the yacht, instead of the doctor.

The weather now looked very settled and there was little chance of bad weather for a time. I gave Pollock his instructions, and left with him, as a crew, Ted Milner and George Spanner. I packed up my traps and pulled off with the others to the bay, not at all sorry to do a little work for a change.

We took Jacko on shore with us. He did not admire the island, and particularly objected to the land-crabs. His favourite amusement was to turn on the tap of our tank, when no one was looking, and let all our hard-got supply of water run out.

He behaved very well on the whole, however, except on Christmas Day, when he drank some rum which he found at the bottom of a pannikin and, I am grieved to say, became disgracefully intoxicated. He had a dreadful headache the next day.

CHAPTER XVII

PICK AND SHOVEL

As it was a Sunday there was no work done on the first day of my stay in camp; all hands had the usual holiday, which they chiefly employed in fishing, and mending their clothes. I walked up the ravine and was surprised to find that so much of the landslip had been already removed. The trench was about twenty feet broad, and ultimately attained a depth of upwards of twenty feet in places. It extended for some distance along the face of the cliff—if that term can be properly applied to a steep slope of a sort of natural concrete, a compact but somewhat brittle mass of stones and earth. It was at the foot of this cliff that we expected to find the cave described by the pirate, but how far we should have to dig down through the accumulation of earth and rocks that had fallen from above and now filled up the bottom of the ravine it was not easy even to conjecture.

Our object, it will be seen, was to clear the face of the cliff until we came to the original bottom of the ravine. Though the cliff was, as I have explained, composed of brittle matter, as if in an intermediate state between earth and rock, and of comparatively modern formation, it was easy to distinguish it from the much looser soil of the landslip that lay along its sides; this last, too, was of a very different colour, being reddish brown, whereas the cliff was slate-blue.

The men had constructed several little paths leading from the trench, down the ravine, to the edges of the chasms and precipitous steps which are frequent in this gully, and the earth and stones that were dug out of the trench were carried down these paths in the wheelbarrows and tilted over the precipices. As we gradually filled up these chasms the roads had to be extended further down the ravine, and at last we had formed a great dyke which stretched right across it. I was satisfied that all the operations had been conducted with judgment, and, if the treasure were in the ravine at all, there was but little doubt that we should find it.

The same rules that had been laid down by the doctor for the discipline of the camp were observed during my stay on shore. All hands turned out at dawn, and cocoa and biscuit were served out. Then we worked hard from half-past five till nine, at which hour the temperature in that closed-in ravine became so high that it was quite impossible even for a black man to work with pick and shovel. A bath in the sea, to refresh ourselves and wash off the clinging red dust, was our next proceeding. Then we put off our working clothes for others, and partook of a good breakfast, consisting chiefly of oatmeal, which we found by experience was the best food to work on. During the heat of the day we lay in our tents, almost panting for breath at times, so intolerably hot and close it was. At half-past three we returned to the ravine and did another three hours' work. After this was another bath, then supper. There was a whole holiday on Sunday and a half holiday on Wednesday.

Even during the early hours of the morning, when the sides of the ravine shaded us from the sun, digging was hot and trying work for white men. We were, of course, bathed in perspiration all the while, and were, consequently, very thirsty, so that the cook was kept busily employed in going backwards and forwards between camp and trench to refill our water-bottles.

In the middle of the day the sun, blazing on the sands, made them terribly hot. No one could step on them with bare feet, even for a moment; one could not even lay one's hand on the ground. The sand here is mixed with a finely granulated black mineral substance, and I think it is the presence of this that causes so great an absorption of heat. I have never found sands elsewhere, even in the Sahara, attain so high a temperature.

We were not altogether lazy out of digging hours. One's clothes had to be washed, water had to be brought down in breakers and demijohns from the distant issue in the cliffs, and firewood had to be gathered. We sometimes went out in a body to perform this last duty. We would climb high up the mountain sides, where the dead trees lay thickest, and throw down the timber before us as we descended, until we had accumulated a large quantity at the bottom.

I shared one of the tents with Purssell, while the doctor and Powell occupied the other. On my first night on shore we caught three turtle. Our black cook, who was always looking out for them, came to my tent and reported that, while prowling about the beach, he had observed several large females crawling up the sands. It was a very dark night, so, taking a lantern, four of us set out. We soon came across one of the creatures, and followed her quietly until she had reached a spot far above high water mark, and then we turned her over on her back. This is by no means an easy undertaking when one has to deal with a seven-hundred-pound turtle, and requires at least four men to carry it out. The turtle does not permit this liberty to be taken with her without offering considerable resistance: with her powerful flippers she drives the sand violently into the faces of her aggressors, attempting to blind them, so that caution has to be observed in approaching her. We turned over three turtle, and, on the following day, salted down the meat that we could not eat in a fresh state.

Turtle are kept alive for weeks on board ship, even in the tropics, and all the care that is taken of them consists in placing pillows under their heads, as they lie on their backs on deck—so as to prevent apoplexy, I suppose—and in throwing an occasional bucket of water over them. These creatures seem to be able to do without food for a very long period. We found that we could not employ this method of keeping alive the turtle we caught, for, though we constantly poured buckets of water over them and shaded them with matting, they could not exist on these blazing sands; and the practice, cruel enough at sea, would have been much more so here.

The paid hands enjoyed turtle-hunting, and were inclined, thoughtlessly, to turn over more turtle than were required for purposes of food; so that I had to give an order that no turtle should be turned over without leave, and the destruction of the creatures was strictly limited to the requirements of the larder.

A similar law was made for the protection of the silly sea-birds, and the only animals that could be slaughtered with impunity were the unfortunate land-crabs, for they had no friends among us to take their part and legislate on their behalf. They were now not nearly so plentiful in the vicinity of the camp as they had been. They had begun to give up their ignorant contempt for man, and on only one occasion during my stay on shore was it considered necessary for four of us to sally forth with sticks, before supper, and slay about a hundred each.

The turtle were now so plentiful that we could have caught in a fortnight sufficient to last us for six months, had we even lived on nothing else. The Trinidad turtle are of large size—500 to 700 pounds—and their flavour is excellent. We had turtle-soup and turtle-steak every day for breakfast and dinner, so that we became utterly weary of the rich food, and I do not think any of us wish to see calipash or calipee for a long time to come.

We did not neglect the other useful products of the island. We gathered the wild beans, and found them a very welcome addition to our diet. Of fish we always had plenty. Powell was our great fisherman, and was the inventor of the seine constructed of wire-fencing which I have already described. In addition to the edible fish I have mentioned as swarming in these waters, there are several other species that we looked upon with some doubt, and refrained from eating. Some of these were of quaint forms and dazzling colours, so that their appearance seemed to warn us of their poisonous nature. There were fish of brilliant blue, others with stripes of white and purple, others with vermilion fins and yellow bands like those of a wasp. Sea-snakes abounded in the pools. These, according to the Italian cook we had on the "Falcon," are edible; but we did not venture to try them. They attain the length of five feet and are of a grey colour, with yellow stripes. They appear to be of savage disposition, for, when harpooned, they twist about and bite with fury anything within their reach.

I stayed on shore altogether for a fortnight, and kept a journal of our proceedings, which, together with several sketches, specimens of the flora, and other articles, were washed out of the lifeboat and lost when we abandoned the island. The loss of the journal, however, matters little, for our life on shore was almost devoid of incident, and was chiefly made up of monotonous work with pick, shovel, and wheelbarrow.

We dug away, still through loose soil that had evidently formed part of the landslip, and removed some thousands of tons; but we did not come to the foot of the cliff, or the cave which is described to be there. Some of the stones that we had to remove in the course of our digging were very large. We had a quantity of strong ropes and blocks on shore, and when we came across an exceptionally big rock, we clapped a number of watch-tackles one on the other, and, by putting all hands on the fall of the last tackle, we obtained a very powerful purchase, equivalent, I calculated on one occasion, to the power of five hundred men. We found bones and bits of decayed wood among the earth, but the former always proved to be the remains of a goat and not of a pirate, and the latter were the fragments of dead trees and not of chests of loot.

But shortly before Christmas there were some encouraging signs. We had now got down to a considerable depth, and we noticed that, when a pick was driven into the bottom of the trench, a hollow sound was given out, as if we were on the roof of a cavern, and, occasionally, little holes would open out and the earth would slip down into some chasm underneath. We dug still deeper, and we came to a collection of very large rocks, which we were unable to move. They were jammed together, and evidently formed the roof of a cavern, for, wherever we could clear away the earth that lay between any two of these rocks, we looked down through the opening into a black, empty space, the bottom of which we could not touch by thrusting through our longest crowbar. This looked promising, for it was just such a cavern as this that we were seeking.

We found that the rocks were too close together to allow of our effecting an entrance from above, so we dug down along the side of the last and largest of these until we came to its foot; and there indeed was a sort of cavern, partly filled up with loose earth, which we cleared out.

There was no treasure in it, and nothing to show that any human being, before us, had ever visited the spot. I think it was at this stage of our operations that each man began very seriously to doubt whether we were searching in the right place at all, and whether there might not be some further clue that was missing, and, without which, search would almost certainly be futile. But, whatever may have been thought, there was, so far as I can remember, no expression given to these doubts, and each worked on with the same cheery will as at the beginning, even as if he were confident of success. These men were determined, in an almost literal sense, to leave no stone unturned, and not to abandon that ravine until they had satisfied themselves as to whether the treasure was or was not there.

On the Sunday after my arrival on shore, December 22, we went off in the whale-boat to see how Pollock was getting on. The weather had been exceedingly fine throughout the week in South-west Bay, and we might have launched the boat on almost any day; but, though there had been no heavy wind in the neighbourhood of the island, there had been a considerable swell at the anchorage for part of the time, and Pollock reported that the yacht had tumbled about a good deal. He had found opportunities for landing at the pier with the dinghy, and had brought off some breakers of water from the cascade and a quantity of firewood. He had been very lucky with his fishing, having caught several germanic, weighing from twenty to forty pounds apiece, and an abundance of other fish. Ted Milner was now taken on shore with us, while Arthur Cotton was left on board.

We worked away steadily in the ravine until Christmas Day, when there was, of course, a holiday. We had a most luxurious dinner on shore, as also had the three men on board the vessel. The menu of our shore-dinner was as follows:—Turtle soup, boiled hind fish, curried turtle steak, boiled salt junk, tinned plum-pudding. For vegetables we had preserved potatoes and carrots, and Trinidad beans. Good old rum was the only beverage. There were some other luxuries, chief of which was a box of cigars, which had been put away for this occasion.

Christmas Day was intensely hot, so that we remained in our tents, having no energy for exploring mountains. With the exception of Jacko's disgraceful intoxication, no incidents of note occurred.

On the Sunday after Christmas Day, Purssell and myself set out to explore the weather side of the island, taking our lunch in our pockets—biscuit, figs, rum and tobacco. We crossed the Sugarloaf Col and descended upon the coast of South-east Bay, then we turned to the right and followed the shore to the extreme south end of the island, where Noah's Ark falls a sheer wall into the surf.

There was a quantity or wreckage in this bay, and in one place we found a topmast and some ribs of a vessel which might have been the remains of the hull I had seen here nine years before. The broken bits of planks, timbers, barrels, hencoops and other relics of ships were piled quite thickly on the rocks above high water mark, and we came across a square-faced gin bottle, full of fresh water, which, from its position, could not have been washed ashore, but must have been left here by some human being. We saw the footprints of turtle, showing that every sandy beach of this island is frequented by numbers of these creatures. In view of the threatened turtle-famine we read of, it might be worth some one's while to come here for a cargo of them; but the difficulty of getting any quantity off alive would be great.

The scenery of East Bay is very extraordinary, for here the signs of volcanic action are more evident than on any other portion of the island. At the south end of the bay there is no sandy beach; masses of shattered rocks, fallen from above, strew the shore, and between these are solidified streams of black lava, which appear to have followed each other in successive waves, one having cooled before the next has poured down upon it, so that a series of rounded steps is formed. The ledges of lava, as will be seen on reference to the plan, extend far out to sea, producing a dangerous reef, on which the sea always breaks heavily.

As we advanced over the boulders there towered above us on our right hand the perpendicular side of Noah's Ark, of a strange red colour, looking like molten iron where the sun's rays fell upon it. A quantity of red *débris* from the roof of this mountain was also lying on the shore, and at the north end of it we observed that a gigantic *couloir*—as it would be called in the Alps—of volcanic ashes and lava sloped down from its summit to the gap which connects it with the Sugarloaf. It was obvious, from the vast amount of these fire-consumed *débris* and waves of lava surrounding its base, that Noah's Ark had once been a very active volcano, and I think it highly probable that there is a crater at the top of it. Though it is perpendicular on three sides, it might be possible to ascend it from the fourth side, by the *couloir* connecting it with the gap under the Sugarloaf; but the attempt would be risky, and a slip on its steep, sloping roof would mean a drop over a wall 800 feet in height.

We clambered over the rocks until we came to the end of Noah's Ark, and we stood on a ledge of lava and gazed at one of the strangest sights of this strange island. The base of the great red mountain is pierced by a magnificent tunnel, known as the Archway, which connects South-west Bay with East Bay. What seem to be gigantic stalactites depend from its roof; and the different gradations of colour and shade on its rugged sides, from glowing red in the blaze of the sun to terra-cotta, delicate pink, and rich purple, and then to deepest black in the inmost recesses, produce a very beautiful effect. The heaving water is black within it, save where the white spray flashes; but, looking through it, one perceives, beyond, the bright green waves of South-west Bay and the blue sky above them.

The sea does not flow freely through the tunnel, except at high water; for, on the side we were standing, its mouth is crossed by a ledge of lava, which is left dry by the receding tide. But inside the tunnel there is deep water, and the ocean swell always penetrates it from South-west Bay, dashing up its sides with a great roar, which is repeated in hoarse echoes by the mountain.

According to an ancient description of Trinidad, quoted in the "South-Atlantic Directory," the Archway is 40 feet in breadth, 50 in height, and 420 in length. I think it far higher and broader than this, at any rate at its mouth. No doubt the action of the surf is continually enlarging it.

Purssell and myself, having admired this beautiful scene for some time, turned back, crossed the rocky promontory of East Point, and proceeded along the sands till we came to the Portuguese settlement, which I wished to examine more carefully than I had been able to do, when here with the doctor a month before.

We had lunch by the side of the river which flows under the Portuguese ruins, and then commenced to explore. The Portuguese had certainly selected the only spot on the island at all suitable for a permanent settlement; for not only is there here the best supply of water, but there is also a considerable area of fairly fertile land, though it is greatly encumbered with rocks. The downs by the river are densely covered with beans, which also grow all over the ruined huts. It is possible that these beans were originally planted here by the settlers, and have since spread over all the downs between this and South-west Bay; for they are not to be found on the other side of the island.

The huts, of which the rough walls of unhewn stone alone remain, are built in terraces one above the other on the hillside. A great deal of labour was evidently expended in the construction of these terraces, and of the roads leading to them, and quantities of stones had been piled up in order to obtain a level surface. This must have been a picturesque little village in its day—whenever that day was for, though I have searched diligently, I can find no record to show what period Trinidad was used as a penal settlement by the Portuguese. Amaso Delano, writing of his visit to the island in 1803, speaks of a "beach above which the Portuguese once had a settlement;" and a still older narrative alludes to a Portuguese penal establishment here as a thing of the long past. Malley, who was here in 1700, took Trinidad in the name of the King of England—as I have already mentioned—and he says nothing of such a settlement.

Near the huts we found places where the soil had been

cleared of stones, for purposes of cultivation, and there were several walled-in enclosures.

We saw a good deal of broken pottery and tiles lying about, not such as we had discovered in South-west Bay, of Oriental manufacture, but of a very rough description, probably home-made. For, on the top of a hill overlooking our ravine, we came across a hole that had evidently been dug for the purpose of extracting a sort of clay that is there, and there were signs of fire near it, and many fragments of earthenware, so we conjectured that we were looking at all that remained of the ancient Trinidad pottery-works.

We did not return to South-west Bay by the Sugarloaf Col, but by another route, which the shore-party had discovered in the course of a previous Sunday's tour of exploration. This lay over the gap in the downs at the back of our bay. It is indicated in the plan, and presents no difficulties; but the soft soil and tangled vegetation make the climb a rather laborious one.

CHAPTER XVIII

A VOYAGE TO MARKET

I REMAINED on shore for a fortnight, during which the weather was fine, though a slight shower generally fell in the morning.

We had still a large supply of stores, both on shore and on board; but there was one article of food which we were consuming in much larger quantities than had been anticipated—the necessary oatmeal—and it was now found that but very little of it was left. It was, therefore, decided that I should sail to Bahia—our nearest market-town—with the yacht, and procure some more.

A voyage of 1,400 miles in order to purchase a little oatmeal sounds like a rather large order; but, as a matter of fact, it was more comfortable to be under weigh than to lie at anchor where we were, exposed to the ocean swell. So we did not look upon the journey as a troublesome duty.

My crew was to consist of Pollock and the three white sailors. I put Ted Milner, the boatswain, on Pollock's watch, and took Arthur Cotton on mine. John Wright did the cooking and kept no watch, though he was always ready to lend a hand if necessary.

On Sunday, December 29, the whale-boat went off to the yacht for another load of stores, so that there might be an ample supply on the island during the absence of the vessel; for it was not possible to foresee how long we should be away.

On Monday, 30th, I returned on board, and, after the two parties had bade each other good-bye and good luck, the whale-boat went off to the shore with a last cargo of provisions. We now got the vessel ready for sea. We unbent the storm-trysail and storm-foresail, and bent the large foresail; being rather short-handed, we left our topmast housed during this voyage.

We did not weigh the anchor until 5 P.M.; we set the whole mainsail, the mizen, foresail, and second jib. The wind, at

163

first, was exceedingly light, so that we drifted helplessly about for a time, and we did not get clear of the island until after dark. I was thus unable to sail round to the mouth of South-west Bay and satisfy myself that the boat had been safely beached. However, seeing that so many successful landings had been accomplished, I considered it unnecessary to hang about the island until the following daylight, so we shaped our course for Bahia. A moderate wind sprang up in the night and we soon left the island far behind us.

This was a most successful voyage. The wind was from the north-east all the time, right abeam, and therefore as favour-able as it could be. There was not quite enough of it, how-ever, and our best days' work was only 154 miles. On one day it was rather squally, and we had to trice up the main tack now and then. The voyage only occupied five days, for we sighted the white sands and the cocoanut groves of the Brazilian coast at 5 P.M. on January 4, and at 7.30 we rounded St. Antonio Point and entered the bay of Bahia. Here we found that a strong tide was running against us, and, as is usually the case in the gulf at this hour, there was scarcely any wind; so we were compelled to let go our anchor near the lighthouse. A Newfoundland barque that had followed us in had to do likewise.

The next day, January 5, we rose early and saw before us again the beautiful white city which we had left nearly two months before. We got up the anchor as soon as the morning breeze had sprung up, and sailed slowly to our anchorage under Fort la Mar, where we let go in three fathoms of water.

We noticed that a strange flag was flying on all the forts and government buildings, as well as on the guard-ship and a little gunboat that was lying near us. It bore no resemblance to the flag of Brazil, or to that of any other nationality, and puzzled us somewhat.

Though it was Sunday, our old friend, the harbour doctor, came off to us in his launch. I was uncertain as to how he would receive us; for the regulations of Brazilian ports are strict, and our entry here was most informal. We had sailed out of Bahia, as the doctor himself must have known, two months before, presumedly for Sydney, Australia; and now, here we were again at Bahia, with no bill of health, and only half of our crew on board.

He came alongside, and we greeted each other. "What port do you come from?" he then asked.

"We have been in no port since we left here," I replied.

"How—in no port!" he exclaimed, raising his eyebrows in slight astonishment. He was too thorough a Brazilian to express much surprise at anything, or to rouse himself from the almost Oriental apathy of manner that distinguishes this somewhat indolent race.

Then I explained to him that we had been passing our Christmas holidays on the desert island of Trinidad, that I had left most of my companions there while I had sailed to Bahia for more stores, and that, having been in no inhabited port, I had, consequently, been unable to provide myself with a bill of health.

"And what were you doing on Trinidad all this time?"

"Among other things, we were making collections of the fauna and flora. There are some rare birds."

"Have you any specimens of the birds on board?"

Luckily I had a few, and exhibited them. He was somewhat of a naturalist himself, and recognised one species which he had seen on Fernando Noronha.

He seemed satisfied, and gave us pratique without any demur.

Mr. Wilson had, of course, seen us, and had sent his boat to fetch me on shore. Leaving the others on board, I got into the boat, and, as the black boatman pulled me under the fort, it occurred to me to ask him, in the best Portuguese I could muster, what was the signification of the new flag that floated above the battlements. In my anxiety concerning pratique I had forgotten to make any enquiries on the subject from the doctor. The black looked up at the flag, smiled faintly, and replied with an indifferent air—"Ah! la Republica."

And so indeed it was—the Republic! When I reached the store, Mr. Wilson told me all about the revolution, which had occurred quite suddenly and quietly on the day after we had last sailed from Bahia. I learnt that the much esteemed Emperor had been deposed, and that a Republican form of government had been proclaimed. And a very shabby sort of a revolution it had been, too, for there had been no slaughter, to give an air of dignity and respectability to it. The people themselves appeared to be heartily ashamed of such a feeble thing, and spoke little of it. The most insignificant Republic of Central America could have got up a far more exciting and sanguinary affair at a few hours' notice. The harbour doctor had not even thought it worth while to mention the change of government when he gave me pratique.

No national flag had yet been selected for this latest addition to the list of American Republics, and the flag we saw was that of the State of Bahia. There had been no disturbance in this city when the news of the *pronunciamento* was telegraphed from Rio. The negroes did not raise a hand to support the Emperor to whom they owed their freedom. The only incident of note that occurred at Bahia was the salute that was fired at Fort la Mar in honour of the new Government. This salute did cause some little excitement: for, by some mistake, round shot were fired instead of blank cartridges, and one shot went through a longboat swinging on the davits of a Norwegian barque, and did other damage.

The United States gunboat "Richmond" was at anchor in the bay, awaiting instructions from Washington, it was said, before officially recognising the new sister Republic.

The next day was the feast of the Epiphany, a great holiday, and no Brazilian could be got to work under any circumstances whatever. Crackers, rockets, and bells were the order of the day. Even for the two days succeeding the festival these pious people were disinclined to work, and I heard the skippers of vessels raving in Wilson's store because they could not get the water-boats alongside, or ship their ballast, as the lightermen were still busy letting off crackers in the streets. However, we managed to get all our stores off—oatmeal, plenty of fresh vegetables, fruit, molasses, and a small barrel of *cana* or white rum.

On Thursday, January 9, I renewed my acquaintance with

some old friends. The telegraph steamer "Norseman" came into the port. She was still under the command of Captain Lacy, who had taken the "Falcon" in tow with her from Rio to Maldonado nearly ten years before.

We had intended to sail on this day, but the glass had been falling and it was blowing hard from the south-east, so that it seemed advisable to wait for some improvement in the weather. The next day, January 10, the glass began to rise, and the sky looked less threatening, the scud no longer rushing across the heavens at a wild pace; so we got under weigh after breakfast, and once more set sail for the desert island.

For a vessel sailing from Trinidad to Bahia the wind is always fair, being from north-east to south-east; but for one sailing the reverse way the wind is, as often as not, right ahead. This bad luck we now experienced. Trinidad lay to the south-east of us, and south-east was also the direction of the wind. When we were outside the bay we put the vessel on the port tack and at five in the evening we were off the Moro San Paulo lighthouse. Then we went about and steered away from the land.

This was, I think, our most disagreeable voyage. It blew hard all the time, and there were violent squalls of wind and rain that frequently compelled us to scandalise our mainsail and lower the foresail. The sea ran high and was very confused, so that, sailing full and by, the yacht made little progress, labouring a good deal, and constantly driving her bowsprit into the short, steep waves. On the third day out we took two reefs down in the mainsail and two in the foresail. The wind was constantly shifting between east and south, so that we often went about so as to sail on the tack which enabled the vessel to point nearest to her destination.

When we had been six days out we were only half way to Trinidad, having accomplished the distance of 350 miles from Bahia.

On this day I had some trouble with Arthur. He had, I think, brought a bottle of rum on board surreptitiously at Bahia, or, possibly, he had helped himself from the barrel, which was always kept, for security, in my cabin. As I used to sleep on deck during Pollock's watch, he could then find his opportunity, as no one was below to catch him. At midnight, when I relieved the other watch, he refused to obey an order. He had done this on two previous occasions, also when under the influence of smuggled spirits, and had quickly been brought to his senses and to his work by having his head punched. It was his wont to become repentant and make amends for his bad conduct by extra good behaviour; and I must allow that he did his work willingly enough, as a rule, but drink converted him into a foolish sea-lawyer.

The offence was flagrant on this occasion, and as a head-punching only resulted in making him sulky, I determined to discharge him. Seeing that months might elapse before we left Trinidad for the West Indies, and not wishing to have him on my hands all that time, I made up my mind to run back to Bahia with him at once; so the mainsheet was promptly slacked off, and we bore away, to the young man's great surprise. I would not let him go below, in case he should get at the rum again; so ordered him to stay on the deck forward. Before the end of my watch he disobeyed this order and sneaked below in the dark. When I discovered this I went down and ordered him to come on deck at once. He obeyed, promptly this time, as he was, no doubt, reaching the sober and repentant stage; but I would not trust him, and tied him up by his foot to the bulwarks forward, and kept him a prisoner until we came into port.

He was the only paid hand we had who was subject to these fits of insubordination. The doctor and myself never had any difficulties with the others; they did their work cheerfully.

Now that we were running before the wind and sea we made good progress, and we sighted the Moro San Paulo light at 2 A.M. on Sunday, January 19. The distance, therefore, that we had made after six days of tacking was now accomplished before the wind in 50 hours.

We were becalmed off the entrance of the bay for several hours. It was an excessively hot day, and the morning breeze did not spring up till later than usual, so that we did not let go our anchor under Fort la Mar until midday. And now, lo!

the flags of the State of Bahia no longer decorated the city and forts, but a flag something like the old Brazilian flag, but yet not the same, floated everywhere. Had there, then, been yet another revolution while we were away, and was some new form of government—communistical or oligarchical or what not—being experimented upon? We learnt, on landing, that this was the National flag of the Brazilian Republic, but only a tentative one, which was being flown so that the citizens could see how it looked. I believe several other patterns were tried, and thus exhibited in the cities for public approval, before one was definitely selected.

The harbour doctor came off to us, was amused at our story, and again gave us pratique. Wilson had, of course, been much puzzled at the re-appearance of the "Alerte," and was anxious to hear what had happened.

I took Arthur before the Consul on Monday morning, and formally discharged him.

New brooms sweep clean, they say, and the new Republican Municipality had decided to clean dirty Bahia as economically as possible, and had hit upon the following ingenious plan. The police were instructed to consider any one, whatever his rank, who was found walking in the streets after bed-time, as a dangerous conspirator, and to promptly arrest him. All men locked up on any night for this crime were sent out the next morning in a gang to sweep the streets. It was interesting, I was told, to observe some gay young Brazilian masher, in silk hat, lofty collar, and pointed patent boots, cleaning a gutter out, with an armed policeman standing over him to see that he did not shirk his work. I was instructed by the Consul to warn any of my men who should come on shore as to the danger of strolling about the city at night.

I did not wish to remain at Bahia one moment longer than was necessary; but I thought it would be well, as we were here, to fill up our water-tanks. But it happened to be another fiesta this day—bells and crackers again!—and the water-boat could not come off. So we had to wait till the following day, January 21, when the water was put on board of us, and in the afternoon we got under weigh.

CHAPTER XIX

HOVE TO

IT was blowing hard on the day of our departure from Bahia, and we sailed down the bay under mizen and head sails, so as to see what it was like outside before hoisting our mainsail.

A high sea was running on the bar, and while the yacht was tumbling about in the broken water, an accident happened to Wright. He was preparing our tea, when a lurch of the vessel capsized a kettle of boiling water, the whole contents of which poured over his hands and wrists, scalding them severely, and causing intense pain; so that we had to administer a strong sleeping draught to the poor fellow, after the usual remedies had been applied to the scalded parts. He was on the sick list for a long time, and was, of course, incapable of doing work of any description during this voyage; though, as soon as he got a bit better, it worried him to think that he was of no use, and he insisted, though his hands were bandaged up, in trying to steer with his arms.

This accident made us still more short-handed. There were but three of us left to work the vessel. Luckily, I had one good man with me, in the person of Ted Milner, who not only did the cooking, but worked hard on deck during my watch as well as on the other, and was very cheery over it all the while, too.

When we were outside, we took two reefs down in the main-sail before hoisting it, and close-reefed the foresail, for it was evident that we were in for a spell of squally weather.

We had better luck now than during our previous attempt at reaching Trinidad, for the wind, instead of being right ahead from the south-east, kept shifting backwards and for-wards between north and east, so that we could always lay our course on the port tack, and could often do so with our sheets well off. But the wind was squally and uncertain, and

for much of the time the sea was rough, so that we were eight
days reaching the island.

At dawn on January 29 we sighted Trinidad, right ahead,
and in the afternoon we were about two miles off, opposite to
the Ninepin rock. It was blowing hard from the eastward,
and the sea was, I think, running higher than on any occasion
since we left Southampton. The surf on the island was far
heavier than we had ever seen it before, and was breaking on
every portion of the coast with great fury.

We now ran before the wind towards South-west Bay, and
the squalls that occasionally swept down the ravines were so
fierce that we sailed with foresail down and the tack of our
reefed mainsail triced well up. We saw that the seas were
dashing completely over the pier, and sending great fountains
of spray high into the air. When we opened out South-west
Bay the scene before us was terribly grand. Huge green
rollers, with plumes of snowy spray, were breaking on the
sandy beach; and the waves were dashing up the sides of
Noah's Ark and the Sugarloaf to an immense height, the cliffs
being wet with spray quite 200 feet up. The loud roaring of
the seas was echoed by the mountains, and the frequent squalls
whistled and howled frightfully among the crags, so that even
the wild sea-birds were alarmed at the commotion of the
elements: for they had risen in multitudes from all the rocks
around the bay, and were flying hither and thither in a scared
fashion, while their melancholy cries added to the weirdness
of the general effect.

And once more we saw before us, high above the sea-foam,
our little camp, with its three tents, and the whale-boat hauled
up on the sands not far off, with its white canvas cover stretched
over it; but we were surprised to see no men about: the camp
appeared to be deserted.

It was, obviously, impossible for the shore-party to launch
the boat with so high a sea running, neither could we approach
within signalling distance of the beach; so that there was no
chance of our being able to communicate with our friends for
the present. I also saw that it would be highly imprudent, if
not impossible, to come to an anchor off the cascade with the

yacht. There was to be no harbour for us just yet, and the only thing to be done was to put to sea and heave to until the weather improved.

We did not anticipate that we should have to wait long for this improvement; but, as it turned out, we had to remain hove to for eight days, before the state of the sea permitted the boat to come off to us, during which time the bananas, pumpkins, and other luxuries of the sort, which we had brought from Bahia for the working-party, began to spoil, and we had to eat them ourselves to save them; so that, when at last the men boarded us, we had but little left for them of the fresh fruit and vegetables which were so grateful to them, though of oatmeal and other provisions there was an ample store.

We soon discovered that it was much better in every way for the yacht to be hove to than to be lying at anchor off Trinidad. To strain at her chain in an ocean swell must be injurious even to such a strong vessel as the "Alerte" is; and, as I have said, we did pull one hawse-pipe nearly out of her on the occasion that the chain got foul of the rocks at the bottom, thus giving her a short nip. Even in fine weather we experienced a lot of wear and tear; for the yacht used to swing first in one direction, then in another, as the various flaws of wind struck her, so that the chain was constantly getting round her stem, and we found that a large piece of her copper had been worn away in this manner, just below the water-line.

Had I fully realised before, the great advantages of heaving to, I do not think I should have ever let go my anchor at all here; but, in that case, I should have been compelled to remain on board all the while, and would not have had my fortnight's stay in camp. To remain hove to off this lee side of the island is a very easy matter. Our method was to sail out to sea from South-west Bay until we had got out of the baffling local squalls into the steady breeze, and then we hove to under reefed mainsail, small jib with sheet to windward, and helm lashed. The yacht then looked after herself; and, as the wind was always more or less off shore and the current was setting to the south, she would drift away about twelve miles in the night towards the open sea, always remaining right opposite our bay, so

that those on shore could see us at daybreak. We divided ourselves into three watches at night, one man being sufficient
for a   atch, for he never had anything to do but look out for
the ˙ ssing vessels. Hove to as we were under such short
canv.ₐs the fiercest squall we ever encountered had no effect on
the vessel, and she was in every way very comfortable.

In the morning we would hoist the foresail and tack towards
South-west Bay, so as to attempt communication with the
shore; if that were impossible, we hove to once more, to drift
slowly seawards; and we repeated this process several times in
the course of a day, before we finally sailed out for our night's
rest on the bosom of the ocean.

We could sail into South-west Bay until we were abreast of
the Sugarloaf, but no further; we were then at least a mile
and a quarter from the camp, and it was difficult to read the
signals of the shore-party at that distance, as the flags they had
with them were of a small size.

To have approached nearer than this would have been a
very risky proceeding; for, though we might have succeeded
in getting some way further in, and out again, with safety,
time after time, the day would most assuredly have come when
a serious accident would have happened. For, as soon as the
yacht had sailed across the line connecting the two extreme
points of the bay, the high cliffs diverted the wind so that it
was only felt occasionally, and then in short squalls, from
various directions; and between these baffling squalls were
long spells of calm, during which the vessel would drift helplessly before the swell towards the surf under the cliffs, or
would be carried by the southerly current towards the lava
reefs off South Point, in both cases at imminent risk of destruction. And even when the squalls did come down to
render assistance, they shifted so suddenly that the sails were
taken aback two or three times in as many minutes, so that all
way was lost, or even stern way was got on the vessel, and one
lost control over her at a critical moment.

The "Alerte" sailed into that bay a great many times without mishap; but there were anxious moments now and then,
and I was always glad to escape out of this treacherous trap

to the open sea, clear of the rocks and squalls, with deep water round, and a comparatively steady wind to help me.

We remained thus, standing off and on, and hove to, uring the rest of our stay at Trinidad. Our anchor was nevei et go here again. We had been lucky with our weather wh n we first arrived at the island, and had successively landed our working-party and stores, and our whale-boat had been beached in South-west Bay a good many times, without serious accident, though very seldom without risk. But now all this was changed. High seas and squally weather were the rule during the eighteen days we remained hove to: for the first eight days, as I have said, we were unable to hold communication with the shore; and, after that, there were but few occasions on which we could beach the boat, and then this feat was generally attended with a capsize, loss of property, and risk of life. But, fortunately, as will be seen, the two days preceding our final departure from the islet were fine, and we were thus enabled to carry off our tents and other stores. Had it not been for this short spell of calm, we should have probably been compelled to leave behind everything we possessed.

The fine season here is in the southern summer—our winter. In winter—especially in the months of June, July, and August —landing on Trinidad is almost always impossible. Strong winds and heavy rains then prevail, while the seas run high. It is possible that the fine weather was now beginning to break up, and that when we sailed from the island—February 15—the stormy autumn season was setting in.

The ship's log for this period presents a monotonous repetition of vain attempts at boating, as the following short record of our proceedings for the first eight days will show. It will be remembered that we arrived off the island and hove to on the evening of January 29.

January 30.—Sailed into South-west Bay after breakfast. Though we saw the camp standing as we had left it, could not perceive any men, neither had we done so on the previous day. Wonder if, for some reason or other, the shore-party have left the island, and been carried away by a passing vessel? Drift out of bay and heave to. In afternoon sail into bay again.

This time are glad to see all the men walking down to the beach. We signal for news. They reply "All well," and "Too rough for boating." We signal that we have brought them some letters from Bahia. When outside bay heave to for night.

January 31.—At dawn ten miles off island. Tack towards island. Sea high; squally. Sail into bay. No signals from shore. We conclude it is too rough for boating, and that the men are at work in the ravine. In afternoon sail again into bay. No signals. Heave to for night, as before.

February 1.—Sail into bay in morning. See the men on shore taking the cover off the whale-boat, as if with the intention of coming off. They drag her down to the edge of the sea. We cannot now distinguish them, so cannot tell whether they have launched the boat or not, or whether they have capsized, or what may have happened. All is hidden from us for some time; then we see them hauling the boat up the beach again. They have evidently abandoned the attempt as too dangerous. Very squally. While hove to, drive a long way from island. In evening, sail towards the bay again and heave to for night.

February 2.—Heavy showers of rain obscuring island from our view. Enter bay in morning. It being Sunday no work is done in the ravine, but the shore-party make many fruitless attempts at launching the boat during the day. We stand in and out of the bay all day, watching the proceedings of those on shore through our glasses. On several occasions the men draw the boat down to the edge of the sea, disappear from our sight for a time, and at last reappear hauling the boat up again. They persevere despite repeated failures. Think they have capsized once at least, as they are baling the boat out on the beach. At last, at 4 P.M., they give up the attempt as hopeless, and hoist the signal: "Impossible to launch lifeboat." We exchange several signals, but find it difficult to distinguish their small flags from the yacht. At sunset we sail out to sea and heave to. Choppy sea. Tumble about a good deal. Stormy-looking sky.

February 3.—This morning very clear; so see distinctly for first time the three rocky islets of Martin Vas, distant about twenty-five miles from Trinidad, bearing east. Sail into bay.

Again several vain attempts to launch boat. Heave to. Drift this night upwards of fifteen miles from island.

February 4.—Sail into bay. Still high surf. A signal flying on shore which we cannot distinguish, so sail somewhat nearer in. Are becalmed under Sugarloaf. Then a squall—then taken aback by another squall—then calm again. We drift towards Noah's Ark, up whose face the sea is breaking fifty or sixty feet high. Another squall; wear vessel and clear out of bay. A very squally day, with baffling winds making it more than usually dangerous to enter the bay.

At last, on February 5, after having made three vain attempts to cross the barrier of tumbling surf, the whale-boat was successfully launched, and we saw her come out safely from the line of breakers at the end of the bay; then the men pulled away towards us, visible one moment as the boat rose to the top of the swell, and hidden the next moment from our sight by the rollers as she sank into the valleys between them.

We sailed into the bay to meet her, and hove to abreast of the Sugarloaf. The boat came nearer, and we saw that the doctor, Powell, Purssell, and the two black men, were in her. It was now thirty-eight days since we had last seen our companions. They all looked gaunt and haggard, and were clad in flannel shirts and trousers, ragged and earthstained from the work in the ravine.

But they were the same cheery boys as ever, as I discovered by the jovial manner of their greeting as soon as they were within hail. "Hullo!" sang out the doctor, "what vessel's that, and where do you come from? I am the doctor of the port here. Hand over your bill of health, that I may see whether you can have pratique."

"And I am the governor of this island of Trinidad," cried Powell, with affable pompousness, from under an extraordinary hat that had been manufactured by himself, apparently out of the remains of old hampers and bird's-nests; "will you do me the honour of dining with me at Government House to-night? I shall be glad to learn from you how the revolution is progressing in our neighouring State of Brazil.

176

I was just on the point of sending out my squadron here"—
patting the whale-boat on the side—"to Bahia, to look after
the interest of any of our subjects who may be there."

It was startling for us to find that these dwellers on a desert
island had already heard of the Brazilian revolution, and we
were still more amazed when they proved to us that they were
well informed as to all that had been going on in the outer
world. We had been looking forward to imparting the latest
news to them, but lo! all that we had to tell was stale to them.
They kept us in a state of mystification for some time before
they revealed the source of this marvellous knowledge, and
the only information that Powell would vouchsafe us on the
subject was to the effect that:—"We found it slow here without
the newspapers at breakfast, and have established telegraphic
communication with England. All the latest racing intelligence comes through the tape in the doctor's tent." But,
before asking any questions we greeted our long-absent friends.
They came on board and had a good square meal, such as they
had not enjoyed for a long time, with red wine, cigars and
other luxuries, and after this we sat down to a long yarn and
an exchange of news.

CHAPTER XX

THE ADVENTURES OF THE SHORE-PARTY

THE doctor and his companions had plenty to tell. They had dug a great deal and had cleared away the landslip, till they had arrived at what appeared to be the original rocky bottom of the ravine. They had found no signs of the treasure, and they had evidently come to the conclusion that there was but little chance of finding it; but they had not lost heart, and were of opinion that it would be advisable to dig for a few weeks more, in the likely parts of the ravine, before abandoning the search for good.

The doctor told me that the surf had been exceedingly heavy recently, and that a storm had completely changed the character of the beach, a sandbank having been formed at some distance from the shore, deep water intervening. He explained to me that this bank was only just awash at low water, and that the sea always broke upon it, ploughing it up, so that sand and water were rolled up together, forming a boiling surf dangerous for the boat to cross.

The adventures of the shore party during our absence, the visit of the man-of-war, and the marvellous escape from drowning of several of our men, were very interesting to hear. Mr. Purssell, as being one of those on shore, can tell the story better than I can, and he has kindly written for me the following account of all that occurred whilst the yacht was away. His narrative commences with our separation on December 30.

After parting with our comrades on the "Alerte," we made haste to get ashore again, as the weather looked threatening and there was every prospect of a rough landing. As soon as we had turned the corner of Treasure Bay we found that the wind was blowing hard right on shore, and that the sea had begun to break heavily on the beach, throwing dense masses of spray into the air, which glistened like silver in the sunshine—a magnificent sight, but one which portended a good ducking for us. However, there was no help for it; we had to make the best of it and get ashore somehow.

We waited for a comparative calm. We allowed three big waves to pass and spend their fury on the beach; the word was given, and we dashed on towards the land with all the force we could put into our oars. On we flew, crossing one sandbank on the summit of a curling wave that broke with a sound of thunder on the next bank. On we pulled with set teeth and straining muscles. "Hurrah!" cried the doctor, "one more stroke and we have done it!"—when, suddenly, we were in the back wash—the water seemed to shrink from under us into the wave that followed—the stem of the boat ploughed into a sandbank, while a huge wall of water rose up behind us, lifting the stern high in the air till the boat stood end on, and the next moment oars, tins, boat and men were rolled over and over each other in the boiling foam.

Our first thought, on struggling to our feet, was naturally for the boat. We found her turned right over and thrown almost on dry land. We hastened to right her, bale her out, and drag her up out of harm's way; then, having collected the oars, stretchers, rudder, &c., which were floating about, we set to work to rescue our provisions. For two hours we dived about in the surf, picking up tins of meat, Swiss milk, and oatmeal, a bag of biscuit utterly spoiled, another of flour reduced to paste, a couple of rifles, and one or two boxes of cartridges. Our two happy-dispositioned coloured men had great fun with the ruined flour, pelting each other with it until their shining black bodies were almost covered with the white paste, and roaring with laughter at each successful hit.

Though we did not abandon the search until nothing else could be found, an inspection showed us that we had lost a good half of the stores we had brought off in the boat. Having rescued all we could, the doctor ordered all hands up to the camp for a tot of rum, which, I need hardly say, we were very glad to get. The most important loss, of course, was that of the biscuit and flour: for it was quite possible that the yacht might be away for several weeks, on her voyage to and from Bahia, and we had only a small supply of these articles on shore; so we had to go on short rations, so far as they were concerned.

Cloete-Smith, Powell, and myself had now been on shore for about five weeks, working steadily all the time, and we were beginning to feel the effects of it—in trainer's language, we were getting horribly stale. The doctor, therefore, decided that we should take holidays on the following two days—Saturday and Sunday—and recommence work on the Monday.

Now that the yacht had sailed we were quite cut off from the outer world, and began to feel very much like shipwrecked sailors, with the exception that we had many more comforts than usually fall to their lot. I suppose it is only in novels that those convenient hulks drift ashore containing just the very things the belated mariners are in want of, for, though we kept a careful look-out, nothing of the kind came our way. Powell, I believe, though naturally a most kind-hearted fellow, would have cheerfully sacrificed a vessel for a few hundred Turkish cigarettes, and we should all have been glad of a change of literature. The library we had brought with us was well thumbed and well read, even to the advertisements. We had a motley assortment. We all became Shakespearian scholars; Bret Harte's poems and the "Bab Ballards" we almost knew by heart; and we came to look upon, as very old friends, characters of all sorts and conditions; among others, Othmar, Quilp, Adam Bede, Lord Fauntleroy, the Modern Circe, and Mrs. Gamp.

On Monday we resumed our digging, with renewed vigour after our two days' rest, and worked steadily at the landslip. After we had thoroughly excavated under the big rock which had been discovered when the skipper was on shore, without result, Powell and myself were sent to examine two or three likely-looking places higher up the ravine, so as not to leave any chance untried; while the others still worked away at the old trench.

On the Wednesday morning our work was stopped for a time by the heaviest storm of rain I have ever witnessed. After the first few minutes the tents were no protection from the water, which quickly swamped them, so we armed our-selves with soap and, going out into the open, enjoyed a glorious fresh-water bath. At the same time we had a view of a splendid waterfall. The rain beating on to the windward side of the Sugarloaf gathered in a deep gully on its summit, and, rushing down, struck a projecting rock, and leaped head-long into the sea, seven hundred feet below. The effect was very fine, and, later on, when the clouds lightened a little and the morning sun shone through the rain, the whole island appeared to be covered with a transparent veil of prismatic colour.

On the following Sunday the doctor and I set off for an expedition into the mountains. On a previous occasion we had noticed a steep landslip of red earth, mixed with cinders that looked very much as if they had been thrown up from a volcano; so we made up our minds to go to the top and see if we could find a crater. Slowly and carefully we crawled on hands and knees up the steep slide, clinging like cats to the side of the mountain, whose loose, charred soil crumbled away beneath us. We reached the summit of the red landslip, and found ourselves on a projecting spur of the mountain where the rocks had fallen away, leaving a great obelisk, seventy feet in height, standing on a narrow ridge, its base crumbling away with every storm, so that it looked as though a push would send the whole mass crashing down on to our camp far below. We could see no signs of a crater. Leaving this ridge, we ascended the mountain behind, and when we reached the top we sat down to rest and get cool under the shadow of a big rock.

From here the view was a grand one. To our right, nearly a thousand feet above us, rose the highest peak on the island. At our feet was Treasure Bay, our camp looking like a tiny white speck, even the great obelisk of rock we had just left appeared insignificant from this elevation, while the sea seemed smooth and innocent as the Serpentine, and the roar of the breakers sounded like a gentle murmur.

Away at sea two vessels were in sight—one a full-rigged ship, not far from the island; the other a barque, just breaking the horizon, with her white sails gleaming in the sunshine. Suddenly, as I watched the nearer vessel, I saw her royals taken in, and, looking to windward, perceived a large black cloud hurrying towards her, the water being churned up under it as it came along. The next moment the vessel was hidden from our sight by the squall of wind and rain, though all the while the sun was shining brightly on our island and not a drop of rain fell near us. The cloud passed by, the brave ship seemed to shake herself after the struggle, the sun shone once more on her dripping canvas, and by the time she had set her royals again and resumed her course, the squall had passed away below the horizon.

About this time we caught plenty of turtle, which formed a very welcome addition to our larder, and they also enabled us to husband our other stores, which were beginning to get low. Biscuit was entirely exhausted, and of flour we had but little, and, though Joe managed to make a very eatable cake out of preserved potatoes, the absence of bread-food was a serious inconvenience. The wild beans that grow on the island were now of great use.

For another fortnight we dug steadily on, gradually getting worn out with the hard work, and seeing our hopes of fortune diminish as, one by one, the likely places up the ravine were tried and found wanting, and the big trench grew deeper and wider without giving any promise of yielding up the golden hoard. The life was dreadfully monotonous, not an incident occurring worth the mention to vary the daily drudgery with pick and shovel. We no longer set out on Sundays and half-holidays for those glorious but exhausting climbs over the mountains, as we had to cherish all our strength for our work; and, after each spell of digging, were glad to rest in our tents, sheltered from the burning sun. However, we kept up our spirits, were cheery enough, and always got on splendidly together.

The yacht had now been away three weeks, and we began to look forward to her return. We kept a good look-out, expecting to see her at any moment turn the corner of Treasure Bay. Just at this time we found considerable difficulty in obtaining fish. The weather had been bad for many days, the wind strong and squally from the north-east, and a heavy surf running on the shore. The effect of this on our sandy beach was to completely change its shape and appearance, and the little pool, in which we used to catch small fish with our wire-netting, entirely disappeared. Moreover, although Powell was energetic, and indeed very often rash, in venturing out on to the rocks with his bamboo rod, the seas now constantly broke right over them, so that another of our food-supplies was cut off.

On Sunday, January 19, we had an unexpected and most welcome visit. As we turned out of our banqueting hall after breakfast, we saw, to our amazement, a large man-of-war standing right into the bay from the south-east. Our camp was instantly a scene of excitement. We got out our glasses and strained our eyes to make out her nationality.

Was it possible that the Brazilian Government had heard of our expedition and had sent a gunboat to wrest our treasure from us and bear us away in chains? As a relief to the monotony of this long expedition we were always chaffing and talking nonsense—a very good plan, too; so we began to discuss the approaching vessel in our usual mock-grave fashion. If she should prove to be an enemy, we said that we would defend our island to the last gasp. Cloete-Smith began to reckon up what forces he had at his disposal. There were the two Englishmen, more or less white: these he called his Light Brigade. He called the two coloured men the Black Watch. There was the monkey too, who could serve as an irregular force to harass the enemy generally—a sort of "gorilla warfare" as I put it—a remark which called forth a severe reprimand from the commander-in-chief. In the armoury department we had three repeating rifles, two revolvers, and a case of surgical instruments. Fortunately we were not called upon to fight, for, when the vessel had approached close to Noah's Ark, we were able to make out the glorious old white ensign of England floating over her stern. We greeted it with a wild cheer.

Presently we saw that two boats were lowered and manned.

Then the doctor gave the order: "All hands shave and prepare for visitors." We turned to with a will to make ourselves comparatively respectable, all the while eagerly watching the proceedings in the bay. We saw the two boats pull close into the shore, and then retire, evidently not liking the look of the tremendous surf. They were then taken in tow by the vessel, which steamed slowly across the bay and disappeared round the west corner, evidently to see if they could effect a landing in the other bay.

In about twenty minutes, just as we had completed our toilet, she came back again, the boats were hoisted on board, and, to our dismay, she steamed away and vanished from our sight round South Point. We were deeply disappointed, and returned to our tents in no amiable frame of mind.

But we had not been deserted, after all; for, three hours later, just as we had finished our midday meal, we perceived four white-helmeted figures making their way down the green slopes at the back of our ravine. We hastened to meet them, greeted them like long-lost brothers, and brought them in triumph to the camp, for glad we were to see fresh friendly faces. As soon as they had refreshed themselves after their long walk, we sat down to hear all the news. Our visitors proved to be the captain, the surgeon, and two of the wardroom officers of H.M.S. "Bramble," which vessel was on her way from Ascension Island to her station at Montevideo. They had sighted Trinidad at daybreak, and, standing in close to examine it, had discovered our tents on the shore. Having found the surf too heavy both in South-west Bay and at the pier, they had steamed round to the other side of the island. Here, after having attempted a landing at various places, they had at last succeeded in getting on shore, and after an hour's walk over the mountains had reached our camp.

Then we, in our turn, explained to them who we were and what we were doing here; and took them up to see our diggings, in which they seemed highly interested, though somewhat amused at our method of searching for fortune.

The officers asked us to go off and mess with them on the "Bramble"—an invitation we gladly accepted. We accordingly set out with them across the mountains, leaving our two black men in charge of the island during our absence. We found that their jolly-boat was in South-west Bay, with five men in her. They had dropped their anchor near a coral reef running out at right angles to the shore, and now they allowed the boat to back near enough to it for one of us to scramble on board at a time, seizing, of course, the most favourable opportunity when the sea was comparatively steady, and hauling the boat off after each attempt, for, had she touched the rock, not much of her would have been left in a couple of minutes.

We pulled off to the vessel, which was lying at about half a mile from the shore. As soon as we were on board the captain gave the order to get under weigh, and we steamed at half speed into Treasure Bay, and the vessel was anchored for the night near the Noah's Ark mountain, in twenty fathoms of water. Then some one suggested cocktails—a most unwonted luxury for us—and we adjourned below for a chat. We found the officers of the "Bramble" most pleasant fellows, and they treated us with the greatest hospitality. They ransacked their private stores for our delectation, and promised to give us a supply of biscuit, some flour, books, and tobacco to take ashore with us on the following morning. They even said, jokingly, that they were sure the "Alerte" had gone to the bottom, and that, if we were tired of digging on the island, they would give us a passage to Montevideo as distressed British subjects. They appeared greatly interested in the story we told of the origin of the treasure, and the account of our voyage and subsequent adventures. In return, they gave us all the latest news. We learnt that there had been a revolution in Brazil, which had broken out on the day after we had sailed from Bahia, and we speculated as to whether it would cause any delay to our shipmates who had gone to Brazil marketing. We also heard that Lord Salisbury had despatched a fleet to demonstrate on the west coast of Africa. We were told that the "Bramble" was to form part of the expedition sent to observe the eclipse of the sun. They had, in short, plenty of news to impart, and it was so long since we had had any opportunity of hearing what was going on in the world that we talked like a vestry meeting till dinner-time.

All our shore-going clothes were on board the yacht, and we were clad in our rough working clothes, with only one coat between us; so I fancy our appearance at mess was a source of great amusement to the wardroom servants. Indeed, all the time we were on board we were evidently objects of considerable interest to the crew; the men seemed hardly to know what to make of us, and to wonder what manner of people we could be who chose for a residence this desolate spot.

After dinner we went on deck, and Captain Langdon produced some excellent cigars, which we thoroughly enjoyed, while listening to a selection of music performed for our benefit by the ship's volunteer fife-and-drum band—a capital one.

We slept on board the vessel, and the next morning our first thought was about landing; we went on deck to have a look at the shore. We saw that the surf was breaking very heavily, and that it would be impossible to beach a boat without running considerable risk of smashing her up. However, get on shore we must, as the "Bramble" could not delay any longer, and had to be off.

So, after breakfast, the books, flour, and other things were handed up in a cask and lowered into a boat, together with a tin of biscuit, and, having bidden good-bye to our generous hosts, we started off under the command of Captain Langdon. As soon as we were near the breakers it was seen that to beach the boat was impossible, so, after a little consultation, Powell determined to try and swim ashore with the end of a rope. We pulled in as close as we could with safety, and then he jumped overboard, with the end of a grass line fastened to his arm, and made for the shore. He got on all right at first, though the strong current had a tendency to set him on the dangerous rocks on the left of the open channel. As soon as he got into the breaking rollers it was evident that he could not take the rope on shore. He struggled bravely on, being dashed on the beach by each wave, and then sucked back into the next wave by the irresistible backwash.

By this time the two black men on shore had seen him, and

they rushed into the water to render assistance. Then Powell, almost exhausted, handed them the rope and just managed to struggle ashore, and he lay down on the sand for a while, dead beat. But we were by no means out of the wood yet. The two men to whom Powell had given the rope were themselves carried off their feet by the big breakers and were washed out to sea. They both let go the rope and tried in vain to get on shore again, for they were much impeded by their clothes. At last Theodosius managed to cling to a rock and hold on to it till a recoiling wave had passed him; then he made a rush for it and succeeded in reaching the land. But Joe could make no way and was carried further out. He was for some time in great danger of drowning, and his cries for help were piteous. But we could not with safety take the boat any nearer to him than we were, for she would have been stove in by the sunken rocks; and, as we could not make him understand that his proper course was, instead of attempting to land through the breakers in his exhausted condition, to turn and swim out to us, the doctor and myself went out to him, and towed him to the boat on a barrel.

We were now no better off than when we had started, for we still had three of our party in the boat and two on shore. It was clear that it was more than a man could do to swim to land with a rope; so we decided to go to the western end of the bay, where a large rock, on which Powell sometimes fished, stood out some way into the sea, and endeavour to throw a line on to it. So we pulled off there, the two men on the shore following us over the rocks. Powell and the coloured man clambered on to this natural pier, and, after several attempts, I managed to throw to them the end of a light line to which a bolt had been attached; we then bent the end of the grass rope on to this and they hauled it on shore.

But now we found that the sea was breaking with such great violence that it would be extremely perilous for a man to attempt to get on shore by hauling himself along the rope: he would most probably be beaten to death on the coral rocks. We, therefore, attempted to work the line to the eastward for a distance of about half a mile, to where the sandy beach afforded a safer landing-place. Powell and Theodosius carried their end of the rope along the shore, while we pulled in a direction parallel to theirs with our end. We progressed but gradually, having to stop frequently to jerk the bight of the rope over the rocks in which it caught.

After about three-quarters of an hour of this work we had nearly got to our journey's end and were beginning to think that our troubles were over, when the rope got foul of a sharp piece of coral and parted in the middle like a bit of packthread. Captain Langdon used no bad language when this happened, but he looked all sorts of imprecations at this inaccessible home of ours. It was now one o'clock, and we had been trying in vain to land for four hours, and, moreover, had lost a kedge anchor and the greater portion of the grass rope; so Captain Langdon decided to return to the "Bramble" to change the boat's crew and get a fresh supply of rope.

We had some lunch and then set off again with two boats, another kedge and grass rope, a light cod-line and a large rocket. We pulled in till we were near the breakers, then one boat let go her anchor, and, the other boat having her painter fast to her, the first was backed in towards the shore until she was right on the top of the rollers, just before they broke. Then the cod-line was fixed on to the rocket, and, as there was no proper rocket apparatus on board, the rocket was held in the hand, while the gunner, who had come with us, applied a match to it. In consequence of some accident the rocket, instead of flying on shore and taking the cod-line with it, fizzed away in the boat, burning off the gunner's moustache and beard before he had time to move his head aside, and then dropped overboard and expended its force in the water. So we had failed again.

The wind, however, had changed by this time, and for a couple of hours had been blowing off shore, instead of on shore, from the south, so that the violence of the sea had abated considerably, and Cloete-Smith decided to have one more try at swimming on shore. He very nearly succeeded in doing so; but the current caught him, and swept him down on the rocks, so he had to return. Then I made another attempt, but with no better success, and we were at our wits' end and were getting worn out with our efforts, when we saw Powell preparing to swim off to us with the end of that portion of the broken grass rope which had remained on shore.

He waited for his opportunity, then dashed into the surf, dived through the breakers, and managed to get out into the deep water safely. We swam off to meet him with the end of another rope, bent them together and swam back to the boat. The rest was easy. We had now got a connection with the shore; for the further end of the rope was safely secured to a rock. One by one we made our way along the rope to dry land, then hauled the stores off with another light line, and, making the shore end of the grass rope fast to a turtle we had caught two days before, we sent it off as a present to the "Bramble."

It was a relief to find ourselves all safe on shore at last. We went up to the tents in a fairly exhausted condition for a much needed tot of rum. The boats pulled back to the ship and were hoisted up; "Wish you good luck" was run up to the peak; we gave her a parting volley from our rifles, and then the gallant vessel steamed away—as it turned out, to take part in another revolution in Buenos Ayres—and we were alone once more.

On the following day we settled down to work again, cheered and refreshed. We had now got a supply of biscuit and flour which we hoped would last us until the return of the yacht, so we were much more comfortable in our minds than before the arrival of the "Bramble." We resumed our life of monotonous digging, and the only event of importance about this time was an accident which nearly proved fatal to Powell. He was fishing one afternoon on the big rock mentioned above, when one of the large waves which sometimes roll in unexpectedly here washed him off his perch into the sea. He was dashed violently on the rocks, and it was only by a piece of wonderful luck that he managed to clamber up again before he was stunned. He was much bruised, and lost his rod, his pipe, and hat—everything, in fact, except his life.

Day by day the work went on, and, as each morning broke,

we hoped it would bring our missing vessel; but when another week went by and still she had not appeared, things began to look serious. She had now been away nearly five weeks, and we feared that some mischance had befallen her. Our stores were getting exhausted, and the weather seemed to have broken up, for there was now always so much surf that the turtle could not come up the sands, and fishing was generally impossible.

Our stores would not last much longer, so the doctor had two days' provisions and a breaker of water put aside, and decided that, if the yacht did not return within a few days, we would put to sea in the whale-boat and stand out into the track of passing vessels, in the hope of being picked up. Friday and Saturday passed and no yacht arrived. We spent Sunday in getting the boat ready for sea. Monday morning broke with half a gale of wind blowing and a terrific surf on the beach, so that it would have been impossible to launch the whale-boat, and about mid-day, just as we had given up all hope of seeing her again, the good old "Alerte" came round the corner, rolling and pitching in the heavy sea under a close-reefed mainsail, small jib, and reefed foresail.

Next morning we ran the boat down to the water's edge and tried to launch her. Two of us got into her and made ready to pull, while the others shoved her off. Then the others jumped in and we pulled five or six strokes, when a huge breaker caught her, lifted her up and turned her right over, rolling us all in a heap on to the beach. We tried again, with the same result, and then gave the attempt up, and went back to our morning's dig, hoping for better luck in the afternoon.

Day after day we tried and always failed. It seemed as if the sea would never go down. Our stores were now all but exhausted and we lived chiefly on the wild sea-birds. Every morning we would climb to a ravine where the birds are in great quantities, and pluck the young, unfledged ones from their nests, their mothers circling round us, striking at us with beaks and wings, uttering hoarse cries, and even spitting morsels of fish at us in their fury. We then took our victims down to the camp, cooked and ate them. The old birds are inedible, and even the flesh of the young ones is, without exception, the most horrible kind of food I have ever tasted.

At last, on February 5, after a week of this sort of thing, we could stand it no longer, and determined to get off somehow. Three times we tried, and each time were swamped and driven back; the fourth time we waited for a lull, ran the boat out, jumped in and pulled away with all our strength. A huge breaker rolled up. The boat stood up on end, hesitated for an instant; one mighty tug at the oars, she righted, and before another wave could catch us we were out of danger, soon reached the "Alerte," and our imprisonment was at an end.

I cannot close this account of our life on the island without saying a word in praise of the two coloured seamen who were left with us. Always willing to work hard and always cheerful and obliging, they tried to make our life as comfortable for us as possible. When the provisions ran short, they would have lived, had we allowed them, on nothing but a few handfuls of rice or cassava, saying:—"You gentlemen eat the meat; me and George, we used to anything, even starving—you gentlemen not. We don't want meat—you do." In saying this, I do not wish it to be thought that I am making any invidious comparison between these two men and the two white sailors whom Knight had with him on board at this time. They also were good men and capable sailors, and had they been ashore with us would, I know, have done their duty well and willingly. They deserved thoroughly the good discharge which Knight gave them on parting.

CHAPTER XXI

WE ABANDON THE SEARCH

THE five men I had left on the island had certainly done their work well. The doctor had made an excellent leader and had organised all the operations capitally. They had toiled hard and had kept up their spirits all the while, and, what is really wonderful under circumstances so calculated to try the temper and wear out patience, they had got on exceedingly well with each other, and there had been no quarrelling or ill-feeling of any sort.

The ravine had been very thoroughly explored, and we felt that there was but little chance of our finding the treasure. It was highly improbable that the massive golden candlesticks of the Cathedral of Lima would ornament our homes in England. It was decided, however, that, if the weather permitted, we should stay here another three weeks or so, and—as we were satisfied that the treasure could not be at the first bend of the ravine—that we should dig in such other spots as appeared suitable hiding-places, and would be naturally selected for the purpose by a party of men landing in this bay.

The shore-party were glad of a holiday on the yacht after all their labours and privations, and no attempt was made to take the whale-boat through the surf again that day. All hands stayed on board for the night, and on the following morning, as the sea was still breaking too heavily on the beach of South-west Bay to permit of a landing, I proposed to my companions that we should take another holiday and go for a picnic on the water. The cook was, therefore, instructed to prepare an especially good dinner, and, after shaking the reefs out of our mainsail, we proceeded to circumnavigate the island, keeping as close to the shore as we were able, so that we could have a good view of the scenery.

We sailed by the different points which we now knew so well —the Ness, the Pier, the Ninepin—and at last doubled North

Point. This extremity of the island is extremely wild and desolate, and is utterly inaccessible. Many of the sharp pinnacles which cap the mountains are out of the perpendicular, and lean threateningly over the sea. I have already explained that the different species of birds occupy different portions of the island: the crags by North Point are inhabited by the frigate-birds and sea-hawks.

We coasted along the weather side of the island, and when we were nearly opposite to the Portuguese settlement the wind dropped and we had to man the whale-boat and tow the yacht seaward; for we found that she was gradually sagging before the swell towards the reefs, on which the sea was breaking heavily. We could not get round the island, so sailed back, before a very light wind, to South-west Bay and hove to as usual for the night.

Work was resumed the next day, and a boat-load of stores was sent on shore. The newly-formed sandbank which I have mentioned appeared to increase and become a more serious obstacle to landing every day. On this occasion the boat again drove her stem into the sand as she crossed this shoal, and the next wave swamped and capsized her, so that boat, men, and stores were tumbling about in the deep water between the sandbank and the shore.

They managed to haul the boat safely up, and, by diving in the surf, recovered a good many of the tins of food. Then the boat returned to the yacht, Joe being left alone in the camp. He did not relish this at all, for like most black men, he was very afraid of ghosts, and had come to the conclusion that Trinidad was a place more than usually haunted by unsettled spirits. He told us that if he were left alone on shore for the night his only course would be to light a ring of fires and sit in the middle, with a tight bandage round his head, keeping awake till dawn. If he failed to take these precautions he would most certainly be torn to pieces, or otherwise seriously damaged, by the spirits. We took compassion on him and did not leave him to face the terrors of the darkness alone. In the afternoon the whale-boat returned to the bay, and Pollock swam on shore to remain with him.

A description of what happened for the next few days would be merely a repetition of what has gone before. The yacht was hove to at night, and sailed about the mouth of the bay all day. The surf was always breaking dangerously on the sands, so that it was impossible to beach the boat, and the men had to swim to and fro from whale-boat to shore, or haul themselves along a line which we had rigged up for the purpose, and which was carried from a rock on shore to a buoy moored with the ship's kedge outside the breakers. We used also to haul the provisions on shore with a line, having lashed them to the bamboo rafts which we had constructed for this purpose.

The weather became so unsettled and the surf was so invariably high that, after a few days, we came to the conclusion that the sooner we left the island the better, and we decided to take the first favourable opportunity for bringing off our property from the shore. The bad season was approaching——if it had not already commenced—and if we waited much longer we might find it impossible, for months at a time, to carry off stores or men. The yacht only remained hove to for eleven days after the shore-party had first boarded us, and during that time the men with me on the vessel were employed in setting up the rigging, rattling down the shrouds, and effecting all necessary repairs.

There was nearly always a high swell running now, which was especially uncomfortable when there was no wind, for then we would often roll scuppers under. For nearly a week it was quite impossible to beach the boat, and all communication with the shore had to be effected in the way I have described above. At last, on February 13, luckily for us, it was exceptionally calm in South-west Bay, so that it would be very easy to carry off our stores.

Such a chance was not to be lost. In the morning all hands went off in the boats, with the exception of myself and Wright, who stayed on board to work the vessel. A landing was effected without any difficulty, and the boats returned with heavy loads, bringing off the hydraulic jack, the guns, the bedding, and other articles.

I, of course, wished to see what work had been done, before giving my final decision as to the continuance or abandonment of our exploration—not that there was any doubt as to what that decision would be, after I had heard the doctor's report. In the afternoon I went off in the whale-boat, and landed on the island for the first time for forty-eight days, leaving the doctor in charge of the yacht while she lay hove to outside the bay. I had not put foot on shore here for so long that I was astonished at the aspect of the ravine, which had been completely changed in my absence by the labours of my comrades.

I stood and contemplated the melancholy scene—the great trenches, the piled-up mounds of earth, the uprooted rocks, with broken wheelbarrows and blocks, worn-out tools, and other relics of our three months' work strewed over the ground; and it was sad to think that all the energy of these men had been spent in vain. They well deserved to succeed, and all the more so because they bore their disappointment with such philosophic cheeriness.

It was, obviously, quite useless to persevere any further in this vain search, especially as the difficulties of landing had so increased of late that our operations could only be conducted at a great risk to life. So the fiat went forth—the expedition was to be abandoned; we were to clear out of Trinidad, bag and baggage, as quickly as we could.

We returned to the yacht with a good load of stores, the condensing apparatus, and the faithful Jacko. After dinner we sailed round to the cascade and hove to off it. I remained on board with Wright while all the other hands went off in the boats and obtained six casks of water to replenish the ship's now nearly empty tanks. This was altogether a most satisfactory day's work, and we were very well pleased with ourselves when we hove to at sunset and drifted out to the ocean for our well-deserved night's rest.

On the following morning—Friday, 14th—we tacked to the north of South-west Bay, and found that, though there was more surf than on the previous day, landing was feasible. The boat went off under the doctor's charge, and the tents and all the remaining stores were brought safely on board. Nothing of any value was left; we not only carried off our own tools, but also the picks that had been used by Mr. A——'s expedition. Only broken wheelbarrows and such like useless articles remained in the ravine. From the vessel the only sign of our late camp that could be seen was Powell's disabled armchair, which he had left standing, a melancholy object, on the top of the beach.

We stowed the heavier tools and stores under the saloon floor, and then sailed again to the cascade. The whale-boat went off to the pier and a quantity of water was brought on board, so that we had a sufficient supply—but not much to spare—for the voyage we now contemplated.

When the watering-party returned we had done with Trinidad; so both boats were hoisted on deck, and a melancholy ceremony was performed: our very ancient dinghy, which was too rotten to bear any further patching, and was not worth the room she used to take up on deck, was broken up and handed over to the cook as firewood.

A tot of rum was served out to each hand, we bade farewell to Trinidad, the foresail was allowed to draw, and we sailed away.

It had long since been decided that, whether the treasure was discovered or not, we should sail from our desert island to its wealthy namesake, Trinidad in the West Indies—a very different sort of a place. The distance between the two Trinidads is, roughly, 2,900 miles; but we knew that the voyage before us was not likely to be a lengthy one, for everything is in favour of a vessel bound the way we were going. In the first place, it was very unlikely that we should encounter head winds between our islet and Cape St. Roque, and from that point we should most probably have the wind right aft for the rest of the way, as the trade winds blow regularly along the coasts of north Brazil and the Guianas. In the next place, by sailing at a certain distance from the land, we could keep our vessel in the full strength of the south equatorial current, which runs at the rate of two or three miles an hour in the direction of our course. We had, it is true, to cross the line once more, with its belt of doldrums; but we knew that we should not be much delayed by these tedious equatorial calms, as they do not prevail on the coast of Brazil to anything like the extent they do in mid-Atlantic; besides which, the favourable current would be carrying us along with it across the belt, and enable us to travel fifty miles or so a day, even in a flat calm.

This kindly current would, indeed, carry us straight to our port, for it sweeps through the Gulf of Paria as well as by the east side of Trinidad, and, as every schoolboy knows in these enlightened days, thence flows round the Caribbean Sea and ultimately emerges from it under another and better-known title—the Gulf Stream.

With the old "Falcon" I had sailed over a portion of this route, accomplishing the voyage from Pernambuco to Georgetown, Demerara—a distance of about 2,000 miles—in ten days, thus keeping up an average of 200 miles a day. At this rate the "Alerte" ought to get to Trinidad in fifteen days; but we were not fated to have such luck as that.

CHAPTER XXII

HOMEWARD BOUND

We had bidden farewell to the wild spot that had been our home for three months, but we did not lose sight of Trinidad for upwards of thirty hours.

We had got under weigh at sunset on February 14. A slight draught from the hills carried us a mile or so outside North Point, when we were becalmed and made no progress at all for many hours; and when at last the north-east breeze sprang up, it was so very light that at eight on the following morning the island was not more than twelve miles astern of us.

Throughout the day calms and light airs succeeded to each other, and at sunset the high peaks were still visible. The same weather continued during our second night at sea, and at daybreak on February 16 we could just distinguish one faint blue mountain summit behind us, the rest of the islet being below the horizon. But the wind now freshened and all signs of the land soon disappeared, and once again there was nothing to be seen round us but ocean.

It was evident that we were not to be favoured with the smart voyage I had anticipated. We had fair winds, it is true, and a fair current, but it was rare that we had fresh breezes, while long spells of calm were frequent, so that we did not double Cape St. Roque till February 22.

Our best day's run up to this point was on the 19th, when we made 182 miles in the twenty-four hours—nothing much to boast of, seeing that the difference between our distance, according to our dead reckoning and that calculated by observation of the sun, showed that we had a two-knot current under us all the while.

At 9 a.m. on February 22, having passed between Cape St. Roque and the Rocas islets—not sighting either—we altered our course from north-by-east to north-west, so as to sail parallel to the mainland, at a distance of about 120 miles from it, and thus benefit by the full strength of the current. Having doubled the cape, we encountered, as we had expected, south-east wind, and were thus able to set our spinnaker.

As we approached the Equator we experienced the usual unpleasant weather of this region: the sky was almost always overcast, the calms were only broken by heavy squalls, and no night passed without vivid lightning; but, so far, there was little rain. It was very close in our cabins, and even on deck the men were languid with the oppressive, muggy heat.

We crossed the line on February 26. We now had a few days of drifting over a calm sea, under a soft drizzling rain, and we were unable to take any sights of the sun. On March 1 the wind veered round to the north for a change, so that we were close-hauled on the starboard tack. This wind, being in the opposite direction to the regular trades, was caused by some local disturbance, and only lasted for twelve hours. This was our sixteenth day out, and we were still nearly 1,200 miles from our destination, which we might have made by this time had our luck been good.

If we only progressed at this rate, our water could not hold out to Trinidad; and though this was no cause for anxiety, as we could easily sail for one of the ports on the mainland—Cayenne or Surinam, for instance—I was particularly anxious not to call anywhere on the way; so the order was given that all hands should be put on rations of water. Our usual rule was to allow the men to use as much water as they pleased, without waste; though all washing had, of course, to be done with salt water.

This order brought us luck, for not an hour after it had been given the whole sky was covered over with one vast cloud, so dense that, though it was midday, it became as dark on the ocean as when dusk is deepening into night. Then it began to rain. Hitherto there had only been drizzle or short showers, which did not afford an opportunity for collecting water; but now it was very different—it poured steadily down as it only can in the tropics, so that, by merely collecting the water in the hollow of the whale-boat cover, we soon filled up every tank and breaker on board, and had a sufficient supply to have lasted us to Southampton, had we been bound there. The order as to rations was at once countermanded, and even washing with fresh water was permitted on this extravagant day.

Delighted as we had been to get all this water, we soon wearied of such excessively unpleasant weather, for not only did it rain in torrents, but every now and again a violent squall would sweep over the sea, so that "Scandalise the mainsail, and down foresail" was a frequent order.

"It looks like breakers ahead, sir," sang out Ted in the afternoon, and we quite suddenly entered into a tract of very disturbed water. The swell was unaccountably high, and the seas were curling over each other and breaking all round us just as if we were in a tide-race or overfall. The water, too, which had up till now been of the usual dark deep-ocean tint, became yellowish brown, and, when a bucket of it was brought up on deck, it was found to be full of a fine powder, like the seed of some grass. As we had not been able to take any sights for some days, I thought we might be somewhat nearer the shoals on the coast than I supposed; so hove to and took soundings, but found no bottom. On tasting the water, it was quite salt, so that these phenomena could scarcely have been caused by the violent stream of the Amazon, which often makes itself felt and sweetens the water far out to sea. It is possible that all this commotion was produced by some volcanic eruption at the bottom of the ocean far beneath us— not an uncommon event in this portion of the South Atlantic. As we sailed through this confused water we found that the vessel steered wildly, as if eddies and contrary currents were driving her first in one direction then in another, while the tops of the steep waves kept tumbling down upon our decks, compelling us to keep all skylights closed; this made still more objectionable the atmosphere of our already unpleasantly reeking cabins, where the wet clothes which we had no means of drying had been accumulating for days. The oppressive closeness of this equatorial climate is spoken of with horror even by those who go to sea on big ships; but it is far worse on a little fore-and-after.

Another peculiarity of this tract of broken water—out of which we soon emerged as quickly as we had got into it—was that it swarmed with fish and other forms of life. Shoals of small fish were dashing about merrily in the spray, while fleets of large pink Portuguese men-of-war—as the sailors call the Nautilus—were floating on the surface. Until we had got into this curious portion of the ocean we had seen very few fish.

After some days of similar uncomfortable weather, we drifted or sailed—when the squalls allowed—into a respectable climate again, and ran before the trade wind at a fair pace. Our best day's run was on March 6, when we made 192 miles. On this day we got into soundings, the colour of the deep ocean changing to the dark green of comparatively shallow water; for we were nearing the coast, so as to make the entrance of the Gulf of Paria. We sighted the mountains of Trinidad right ahead of us at daybreak of March 8, about two leagues distant. We ran, before a light wind, between Galeota Point and Baja Point. The sun now blazed down out of a cloudless sky, the morning mists lifted and disclosed the scenery around us, which was of a very different nature from that we had left on the desert Trinidad.

We were no longer tumbling about on the great transparent green rollers that perpetually break upon the coasts of our Treasure Island, but sailing on the smooth, muddy water of a shallow inland sea. On our left were the low shores of Venezuela—a long line of dreary mangrove swamps that form the delta of the Orinoco; the peculiar, and, I should say, somewhat malarious, odour of the steaming mud being plainly perceptible for leagues out to sea.

On our right were the shores of Trinidad—one of the fairest islands of the Caribbean Sea. The sandy beaches were fringed with cocoanut palms, and behind rose gently swelling mountains, covered with fine forests, the lordly palmistes towering above all the lesser foliage—forests in which the trees were of various forms and tints, presenting a beautiful appearance, the feathery bamboos and the scarlet and purple blossoms of bougainvillea and other flowering trees relieving the dark green slopes of dense vegetation. On the plains that lay under the mountains, and in the broad valleys that clove them, could be seen the pale green spreads of the sugar-cane plantations, with the tall chimneys of the boiling-houses rising above them, and the darker clumps of the cacao groves.

When we were near Point Icacos we saw a school of whales, but, not having the whale-boat or gun ready, we did not go in chase.

We passed through the narrow Serpent's Mouth, and were inside the Gulf of Paria; from here we coasted along the shores of Trinidad by many a landmark familiar to myself, and still more so to our two coloured men, who became quite excited when they once more beheld their native islands after an absence of two years and more. We sailed by Cedros Point; by the curious row of rocks that are known as the Serpent's Teeth; by the village of Brea, off which several vessels were lying at anchor, loading with the bitumen that is dug out of of the famous Pitch Lake about a mile inshore.

We did not reach Port of Spain this day, for the wind fell away, and we had to come to an anchor off St. Fernando for the night; but on the following day, March 9, we completed our voyage, and let go our anchor off Port of Spain early in the afternoon, having been twenty-two days out from our desert island.

We were anchored at about two-thirds of a mile from the jetty, and there was only eight feet of water under us at low tide. As the draught of the "Alerte" is ten feet, she then sank two feet into the mud. This is quite the proper way to do things at Port of Spain. Sailing-vessels bound here with timber are in the habit of running as high up as they can into the mud, knowing that when they have discharged their cargo they will easily float off again. The mud deposited in the Gulf of Paria by the outflow of the Orinoco and its tributaries is the softest possible, and is very deep, so that a vessel can suffer no injury by lying in it, even when the sea is rough. So shallow is the water in this roadstead that at a mile and a half from the shore the depth is only three fathoms, while a ship's boat cannot approach the end of the jetty at low water.

I had visited Trinidad before, and had many friends here, so was at once at home on shore, as, too, were, very soon, my companions. We were made honorary members of the pleasant Port of Spain Club, and were treated everywhere with that hearty hospitality for which the West Indies have always been noted.

Our voyage was now over, and though most of my companions were anxious to sail away with me in search of any other treasure we might hear of on West Indian cays—or to turn our vessel's head southward again, and make for Demerara, to travel inland to the gold districts of Upper Guiana on the Venezuelan frontier—or, in short, set sail for any part of the world that promised adventure and possible profit (I believe they would have turned filibusters if the chance had presented itself)—and though I had four paid hands on board also willing to have gone anywhere we should choose to lead them—still, I could not see my way to extending the voyage any further for the present, and decided to lay up the "Alerte" at Port of Spain.

It was with reluctance that I made up my mind to do this; for the men we did not want had been weeded out, and I had round me a compact crew of seven, tested and trained by their seven months' travels and hardships, and I also had the right vessel for any adventure. I had several reasons for laying up the yacht in the West Indies, instead of sailing her home. I had no use for her in England, and, should I undertake another voyage similar to the last, Port of Spain would be a most convenient place to start from; besides, stores are cheap there, and an excellent coloured crew, well adapted for work in the unhealthy tropics, can be readily procured. Moreover, if I decided to sell the yacht, I was certain to get a better price for her in the West Indies, or on the Spanish Main, where there is a demand for this sort of craft, than at home, where the market is glutted with second-hand yachts.

Before leaving Trinidad—that cosmopolitan island of Britons, Frenchmen, Spaniards, East Indiamen, Chinamen, and negroes—we undertook several pleasant little voyages with the yacht in the neighbourhood of Port of Spain, taking with us several friends from the shore. One of these voyages took place in the Easter holidays, which are properly observed on this island. We had a merry party on board, and visited several of the beautiful bays on the islands that divide the Bocas, or northern entrances to the Gulf of Paria. Our crew had by that time been reduced to myself, Mr. Purssell, and John Wright: for my companions took opportunities of returning home as they occurred.

When the old vessel was dismantled and laid up, we last remaining three took passage on the Royal Mail Steamer "Dee," which, being an extra-cargo boat, was bound on a sort of roving commission round the West Indies, in search of bags of cacao to complete her cargo. This was a most enjoyable voyage, thanks to the officers of the "Dee." Purssell and myself were the only passengers. We visited several of the Windward Islands—old friends of mine, most of them—before sailing across the Atlantic to Havre, and thence to London Docks.

Thus ended our treasure-hunting expedition—a vain search; but, as I have already said, my companions bore their disappointment well. It was amusing to hear them argue, like the grape-loving fox in the fable, but in a more good-natured way, that we were far better off without the treasure. I remember one favourite argument to this effect. It had been decided that, if the treasure was found, we should not return to England in the yacht, but insure our wealth and go home in the biggest mail steamer we could find. That was our great difficulty—how to find a suitable vessel. As we were now, we cared not much what sort of a craft we sailed in; but, once wealthy, how terribly valuable would our lives become! In anticipation even of it we became nervous. Would any vessel be large and safe enough for us then that we were millionaires? Well, indeed, was it for us that we had not found the pirates' gold; for we seemed happy enough as we were, and if possessed of this hoard our lives would of a certainty have become a burden to us. We should be too precious to be comfortable. We should degenerate into miserable, fearsome hypochondriacs, careful of our means of transit, dreadfully anxious about what we ate or drank, miserably cautious about everything. "Better far, no doubt," exclaimed these cheerful philosophers, "to remain the careless, happy paupers that we are."

"Do you still believe in the existence of the treasure?" is a question that has been often put to me since my return. Knowing all I do, I have very little doubt that the story of the Russian Finn is substantially true—that the treasures of Lima were hidden on Trinidad; but whether they have been taken away, or whether they are still there and we failed to find them because we were not in possession of one link in the directions, I am unable to say.